MY
REINVENTED
LIFE

My Reinvented Life

The book information is catalogued as follows;

Author Name(s): Eleni Anastos

Title: My Reinvented Life

Description; First Edition

1st Edition, 2021

Book Design by Lynda Mangoro

ISBN (hardback) 978-1-913479-97-8

ISBN (paperback) 978-1-913479-99-2

ISBN (ebook) 978-1-914447-06-8

Published by That Guy's House

www.ThatGuysHouse.com

MY
REINVENTED
LIFE

Finding Purpose in the Pain

ELENI ANASTOS

The force of nature in my life was
my mother, who always said, "Every day
you wake up is a chance for a dream to
come true." This book is dedicated to you,
Lula, for without you, this dream would
never have come true for me. Thank you
for teaching me to NEVER
give up!

CONTENTS

INTRODUCTION

I didn't come this far, to only come this far!

That phrase seems especially fitting during these challenging times (we are in month six of the pandemic as I write this). One of the many things that 2020 has reinforced is that change is inevitable, and reinvention is a vital part of navigating that change to move forward.

Hi, my name is Eleni, and I have had to reinvent myself countless times over the years. The catalyst has often been a painful experience, and I have come to learn that there can be "A Purpose for the Pain." For me, it has become my personal path to reinvention.

I remember when I first heard the phrase, "Life happens for you, not to you," I couldn't have been more annoyed. OK, I was angry. I kept thinking, how on earth could a painful experience that makes me feel sad and hurt or frustrated, be happening FOR me? Gratefully, although it was FAR from easy, I learned to embrace that there was something for me to learn that would help me going forward, even in those difficult moments.

I am a coach, and it is my mission to help people live their best lives, personally and professionally. The path to get there is anything BUT a straight line and requires a degree of reinvention.

I know we all have a story, and countless people have overcome unbelievable obstacles and challenges, have achieved success and experienced the many highs and lows of life. And I hope that you all acknowledge and honor yourself for all that you have been through, all that you have overcome, and all that you have accomplished.

But, have you asked yourself if there is something else, something more you desire? Do you want to add another chapter to your book of life? And please, please don't let anyone else write your story.

On some level, we are always reinventing ourselves, but are you doing it in a purposeful way? So, I will ask again, is there something else you want to be, do or have? Every day, every obstacle, every moment (even seemingly insignificant ones) brings opportunities for reinvention.

Have you ever received a meal in a restaurant that wasn't satisfactory? It could be a catalyst for change, change within yourself. Thus far, you may have been someone who would accept it (while being disappointed), but in that moment you can reinvent yourself as someone who has the confidence to ask for something more.

I grew up in the restaurant business and fondly recall my grandfather often stating, "We're only as good as our last meal." We were taught to constantly "better our best." It is not about competing with someone or something outside of you, but rather evolving into the best version of yourself.

Technology is constantly updating with newer, more advanced versions. That does not mean the original version doesn't function at all; it is simply an opportunity to be even better than before, especially when dealing with painful experiences.

Are you willing to grow through what you go through?

Purposeful reinvention is the foundation to living your best life!

In this book, I will teach you how to reinvent yourself, so you can become the best, most empowered version of yourself that you've ever been thus far!

I will share the themes, experiences, tools and exercises that have enabled me to live a more empowered life.

I reflect back on times when I was healing, felt vulnerable, struggled with boundaries, didn't own my worthiness, felt like it was too late to start something new, struggled to feel gratitude, wondered why I didn't have more abundance in my life or had difficulty forgiving myself or someone else. Although often painful, each of these scenarios served as opportunities for me to become renewed.

Join me on the journey of using the painful experiences we encounter, whether large or small, as the pathway to reinvention, becoming an even more empowered and advanced version of yourself. It's not just feeling the pain but putting it to work and using it as fuel to propel you forward.

Let's all grow through what we go through!

Welcome and embrace the 2.0 YOU!

THE DAY THAT CHANGED MY LIFE

"One wrong blow to the head could have killed me." That thought kept running through my mind as I sat in my living room wearing a neck brace and battling excruciating pain. It all seemed so surreal. Life can change in an instant, and fear can be paralyzing. How did this happen?

It began as a beautiful fall day in Michigan with the alarm going off at 5:30 AM as usual. To be an effective teacher, I needed a certain amount of structure in my day. I always got out of bed quickly, not needing the snooze alarm effect, because I wanted to give myself time to get ready for the day, while still feeling relaxed. I reviewed my lesson plans, ate breakfast and headed to school, arriving shortly before 7 AM. It was "Spirit Week," which leads up to the Homecoming Game and Dance. You could feel the energy and excitement while walking through the halls.

Pep Rally assemblies were a regular part of Spirit Week. The entire high school headed to the gym and the classes (Freshmen, Sophomore, Junior, and Senior) were assigned specific sections in the bleachers. Teachers were also assigned specific sections to monitor. I was assigned the Senior section on the main floor. Most of the 1,600 students came running enthusiastically into the gym cheering, jumping and high-fiving one another. When students settled into their bleacher sections, the cheers grew even louder. It was easy to see how excited they were to be celebrating another Spirit Week Assembly.

I have chaperoned countless Pep Assemblies throughout the years, but I had no idea that today's would be my last. The Pep Assembly included acknowledgement of athletic teams, cheerleaders, the school band and also included various competitions between the classes, including a group cheer. The Freshmen were called on first. They stood up (while remaining in the bleachers) and shouted out the designated cheer, loudly and enthusiastically. A panel of judges from the staff scored their efforts. It was easy to see that the students involved in the competition were giving it their all, wanting to be voted the best. Then it was on to the Sophomores, Juniors, and Seniors. The energy and intensity seemed to elevate with each class.

I remained at my assigned post at the base of the bleachers in front of the senior class. When the seniors were given their turn to cheer, dozens of students came rushing out of the bleachers. It happened so quickly, like a wave crashing onto shore. I got knocked down and trampled. Did they even see me? Was I simply in the wrong place at the wrong time? A victim of circumstance? Before I knew it, I was on the ground struggling, begging for my life. Many of the students that rushed out of the bleachers did not keep moving, but rather gathered around me, violently kicking and stomping on me. I was repeatedly kicked in the back, head, neck and stomach. Each time I tried to get up, I got knocked back down. I was screaming and pleading for help. I was so scared.

I recall having the awareness in the midst of the struggle, that one wrong blow to the head could end my life. I did my best to protect my head with my hands and arms, while still trying to get up and move, again, each time, getting knocked back down. I truly feared that this could be my last day on earth.

A senior student also on the gym floor, but several feet away, witnessed what was happening and reached in to help me. He literally dragged me out of the mob, saving my life. He helped me get up on my feet. I was crying, sobbing, and very shaken. Another teacher saw me in distress and came over, helping me to walk away from the students towards one of the exits, where a couple of administrators were standing. I was then escorted to my classroom, still crying uncontrollably and in extreme physical pain. I was shocked and scared. I told the principal and assistant principal what had happened. They asked a teacher to drive me to the closest hospital and said they would meet me in the emergency room.

When I arrived at the hospital, I asked the nurse to call the police because I wanted to file a report. Part of me was definitely in shock and still couldn't believe this had happened.

I was placed in a room and then examined by a nurse and doctor and taken for x-rays. The x-ray technician asked me what happened. I was still crying as I recalled the assault. I pleaded with the technician to give me the results of the x-ray. I just wanted someone to tell me I would be OK. He told me the doctor would share the results, but I couldn't stop crying. I asked him again. The technician then gently placed his hand on my arm and said, "I can tell you that there are no broken bones." His compassion allowed me to exhale, but only for a brief moment. I remember feeling like it was a very bad dream, and hoping I would wake up and not be hurting or scared anymore. By the time I was brought back to the room, the school administrators had arrived. The sheriff arrived shortly thereafter.

I was lying in the hospital bed, in excruciating pain, wearing a neck brace and thinking, "All I did was go to work like I had done countless times before." I told the sheriff I wanted to file a report and was instructed to handwrite my statement. I was far too shaken to write, so I dictated my account and a fellow teacher recorded it for me, while still in the emergency room.

After a few hours, I was released from the hospital, wearing a neck brace, as doctors were concerned about further injury to my neck. A teacher drove me home and helped me inside the house. I was sitting on my couch, writhing in pain and feeling so scared and shocked, just wanting to wake up from this nightmare. That 5:30 AM alarm seemed like light years ago. I got up and went to work (work I truly loved) and came home in a neck brace after being assaulted. What happened that day? It was supposed to be like every other assembly and day of teaching, and it turned into the "day that changed my life."

Chapter 1
HEALING

"All healing is first a healing of the heart."

– Carl Townsend

HEALING

I was home, staring at the walls, still trying to make sense out of what happened just twenty-four hours earlier. I felt confused and frightened. How did I end up injured, needing a neck brace, when all I did was go to work, like countless days before?

I recall, as a child, often saying to my mother, "I know nothing is going to happen to me that God and I can't handle together." I believed I would always find a way to heal. But this?

This still didn't make sense. I didn't even know those students, never had them in class. The phrase "being in the wrong place at the wrong time" had profound meaning for me now.

My mind was racing, and yet I felt frozen in time.

A few days passed, and the pain in my neck and back did not dissipate; in fact, it became worse. I grew more concerned about my injury and decided to reach out to my chiropractor. I lead a healthy lifestyle, including regular exercise and periodic chiropractor visits to maintain optimal health. When I was in the exam room recalling the incident and my subsequent pain, the doctor was understandably quite concerned. After he examined me, the doctor scheduled an MRI. The results showed I sustained herniated discs in my neck. What? I go to work and come home with a neck injury. A victim of circumstance. It still seemed surreal.

I immediately began questioning the chiropractor. "How do I heal?" "How do I fix this?" I felt there must be a way. I didn't want to imagine remaining in pain and not being able to lead my normally active lifestyle. After also being examined by orthopedic doctors, it was determined that the best course of action for me was physical therapy. My physical therapist came highly recommended, and I felt safe in her hands. I desperately wanted to heal my neck, in part because I, of course, wanted the pain to stop, but I also didn't want to have a constant physical reminder of the assault. I prayed every day, "Please, God, help me heal my neck."

And then there were the emotional and mental wounds which were still quite raw. I wasn't sure where to begin that healing journey.

I knew I hurt. I knew my life was forever changed. I knew I had to heal, but I felt so stuck. I didn't know how I was going to move through this.

Isn't it always easier to process or understand a physical issue than something that is emotional or mental? The level of pain can be the same, in fact – quite intense – but feel and manifest so very differently.

I recall going to see a doctor for a check-up regarding my physical progress. The hospital was only a few short miles from the school. In fact, it was the same exit off the expressway, but in the opposite direction. As I slowed down my car towards the exit, my breathing suddenly became very quick and labored. I soon struggled to catch my breath. My hands were shaking, even as I clutched the steering wheel. I began sweating. What was happening to me? I felt like I was on a runaway train. I couldn't stop reliving the assault. In that moment, I felt the fear was more powerful than I was.

PTSD is real. Depression is real. But how do you deal with it when you can't always see what is wrong? How would people respond? How would I respond?

I was constantly looking over my shoulder, worried I would see someone connected to the assault. I remember going grocery shopping and carrying my bag out when I recognized someone from the school. My heart started racing. I froze for a moment, then dropped my bag of groceries in the parking lot and ran to my car. No one could see the wounds that made me run, but they were very real and deep.

I hated being victimized, but I hated feeling like a victim even more. And, I was even angry at myself because I didn't know how I was going to heal and move forward.

I couldn't work. I couldn't even open the blinds in my house because I feared seeing someone on the other side. PTSD can be so paralyzing on all fronts.

It is my belief that the district purposefully hid the facts of the event. These thoughts weren't helped by various people calling me anonymously to share their own personal traumatic experiences that they said occurred in that school and district. While I was so very saddened to hear their stories, I also felt a strange twinge of camaraderie and connection. I literally felt like I was living through a conspiracy theory movie. How could they say these things never happened? The principal and assistant principal were standing next to my bed in the Emergency Room, but it never happened? I felt like I was being assaulted all over again. When my sick days ran out, I was cut off financially. Thankfully, I was able to live off my savings for several months, but when that ran out, I eventually lost my house and really struggled, especially emotionally and mentally. And, isn't "lost my house" a ridiculous phrase? I know exactly where my house is, I just couldn't afford to live there any longer. I was raised with a strong work ethic and was always proud to be able to support myself. But, when you see that foreclosure sign duct-taped to the front door, no one cares about your strong work ethic, especially the mortgage lender.

I was shocked and couldn't believe this was really happening. I was very committed to my teaching, loved my work and enjoyed helping students. I was a class sponsor, chaperoned dances, attended school sporting events and had been selected as "Teacher of the Year."

And now I felt trapped in a victim mentality. I couldn't see how to move forward with my life.

When I was focusing on the physical pain and wondering how I was going to put gas in the car or food on the table, I became even more frustrated and angry and depressed. You cannot heal in that headspace! And if you can't heal, how do you move forward?

I believed the whole situation was so unfair and got caught up in a vicious cycle of negativity. I could barely recognize myself. Most of my days were spent in fear, frustration and bewilderment. What happened to the positive, proactive and upbeat person that loved and enjoyed life? I couldn't even imagine a happy future, which truly frightened me because I always saw myself as a strong individual who could triumph over anything.

Remember that young child who often told her mother, "Nothing is going to happen to me that God and I can't handle together"? And now, I saw myself as a victim, unable to move forward.

I began praying more, praying for an answer that would help me heal and move forward. I wanted to access my faith that had served me well for many years. I have to admit that I thought my faith was completely gone. Then I realized that you cannot lose faith, but it can lie dormant. Faith is a muscle! Like any muscle, it needs to be exercised to be strong. I focused on reconnecting my faith and spirit with God. I prayed for guidance. Slowly, very slowly, I felt a small glimmer of hope.

A seed of strength began to grow inside of me. I can deal with this. I will deal with this.

There was a part of me that wanted to fight, really fight back against the injustice of it all. Being cut-off financially from the school district also meant I was without health insurance. So, I was unable to continue to get proper treatment for the injuries sustained during the assault. I eventually found an attorney who was willing to help me fight and was determined to "right the wrong."

I was sitting in a courtroom in the state capital, with a judge and state's attorney, fighting to get my health insurance reinstated. I recall the judge stating, "You are a very credible witness, and we believe your story." I replied, "It is easy to be credible when you speak the truth." But the judge said, "Your claim is denied because you've gone against medical advice, refusing to take the psychotropic drugs recommended for PTSD and situational depression." I could not believe what I was hearing. It was surreal. I knew exactly why I had the PTSD and depression and was getting help that felt right for me to deal with both. I chose not to take the pharmaceutical route to deal with those issues, while fully respecting that it may be the right course of treatment for many individuals. When the judge made that statement, I asked, "Since when does an educated, intelligent adult NOT get to decide what does or does not go into her body?"

I was crying so hard in the courtroom that I could barely see. Part of me felt frozen in time, and yet part of me felt like I was on a runaway train. So many emotions ran coursing through my body. It took every ounce of energy and strength I had to appear in court that day. How could the judge believe me, but still deny my claim? It just didn't make sense. I remember looking at my attorney in disbelief. I was fighting so hard for some kind of justice, only to be defeated one more time. It was in that moment that I realized it wasn't about winning or losing – it was about letting go to go on. I couldn't control the court's decision, but I could control my response to it. I felt like I was already robbed of so much, and I wasn't going to allow them to rob me of my ability to choose and move forward. It was time to take my power back and release the victim mentality that had been holding me hostage. It was time to heal.

Regardless of what happened in my life, however devasting, including the loss of loved ones, I was always driven by the attitude of "I will get through this, I will move forward," and didn't always allow myself proper time to process the emotions or truly even grieve. But I also never allowed myself to remain in a victim mentality (or so I thought). I had put my energy on moving forward, not healing the core wound. However, I believed I was healing by being solely future-focused.

It turned out I was setting myself up to engage in an emotional cha-cha ... three steps forward, two steps back.

There were countless times (my brother and mother's passing, the ending of romantic relationships, etc.) I thought I had healed, but I was just being the quintessential "pick yourself up by the bootstraps" kind of woman. A persona I wore like a badge of honor. Can you relate?

If you don't heal properly and only look for a

temporary fix, the shit is going to keep coming back to bite you in the ass. Situations, people and events will keep showing up in your life to let you know there is still work to be done. The emotional cha-cha will continue.

It also means you are choosing to remain a victim.

This epiphany became glaringly apparent as I struggled to heal from the school assault. Not a simple task for the warrior I believed myself to be. I should be able to handle this on my own ... or so I thought. When I realized I couldn't heal on my own, I let shame and guilt creep in. There must be something wrong with me if I can't take care of myself. This attitude only served to perpetuate the victim mentality.

Shame and guilt thrive in secrecy, in the dark.

Shine a light on it, and you take away its power.

Admitting that you are wounded and WANT to heal is an act of courage. Admitting that you need help healing is a huge step in releasing your victim mentality.

When stuck in a victim mentality, there is no growth; in fact, you regress.

You stop being a victim when you take a stand for yourself.

How many times was I just looking for a bandage to stop the bleed, instead of really working to heal the wound?

You might move forward to a degree, but real growth is not sustainable without real healing. And real healing cannot happen when you are firmly planted in the victim mentality. You may have been horribly victimized through no fault of your own, but it is ALWAYS, always your choice to remain in the headspace of a victim.

I now know that healing happens in layers. The decision to heal can happen in an instant, but the process takes time. A tumor could be removed, but your body does not completely heal in that instant.

Healing happens over time. Healing happens with support.

You may not get over something, but I believe you can get through it.

How do you know if healing has taken place?

It is easy to see when a physical wound has healed, but how can you know if your emotional wound has healed? And when should you share your story?

I asked myself those questions regarding my own healing journey. I recalled the countless times I shared the school assault story and subsequent aftermath. Whether I was speaking with a friend, doctor, or therapist, I reflected on who I was being and what my energy and emotional state were like in those moments. It was as if I created a healing timeline to help me gain perspective. When I was extremely emotional, often in tears, it was always closer to the beginning of my healing journey. When I spoke of the assault during those times, I felt I was getting knocked down and stomped on all over again. I went right back to being on the gym floor, begging and screaming for my life. I could see myself hanging onto the victim mentality, still feeling as though the wounds were quite raw and angry at the injustice of it all. Why did this happen to me? Why would they be so cruel?

The reality is you may never know the real reason why something has happened to you. But, you can still move forward. That will always be your choice. Again, true healing cannot happen when stuck in a victim mentality.

When I saw myself talking about the assault without intense emotional charge, I was much farther along on the healing journey. I could feel my resilience growing with each conversation, and I saw myself becoming empowered, having moved forward with my life. I was no longer on that gym floor. I had risen above the trauma.

Share your scars, not your wounds.

A few years after the school assault, a friend introduced me to Notes from the Universe by Mike Dooley. He had a very positive and uplifting way of writing. I decided to attend one of his personal development conferences. I loved being around the energy of people who were committed to their own personal growth.

I especially enjoyed listening to the multiple speakers, sharing their personal stories. It reminded me of my love for public speaking. While teaching, I hosted numerous programs, often speaking in front of 200 to 300 people. I knew in my soul it was time for me to share my voice and story.

I applied to speak at the next conference and was thrilled when I received word that I had been selected. Even though I was also nervous, I felt no hesitation about moving forward. You see, in my application, I had to submit my proposed speech. I referenced the school assault, my healing journey and how I moved on with my life. It was time to share. My real desire to share was and still is to inspire and motivate others to move forward with their lives.

I fondly recall being on the stage, holding the microphone and looking out at the many faces in the audience. I was speaking my truth, and it felt so empowering.

A woman approached me after I was done speaking. She took my hands and looked at me quizzically, repeating, "I just don't understand." I asked, "What don't you understand?" She said, "You were horribly victimized." I said, "You understand that perfectly." She then stepped back, looked at me once again and said, "But nothing about you says victim." I said, "You understand that perfectly as well because that's my choice."

Share your scars, not your wounds!

"The degree to which a person can grow is directly proportional to the amount of truth he can accept about himself without running away."

– Leland Val Van de Wall

What is one thing
you need to heal from
that could make a
difference in
your life?

Chapter 2
VULNERABILITY

"Owning our story can be hard, but not nearly as difficult as spending our lives running from it."

– Brené Brown

VULNERABILITY

Prior to the school assault, I viewed myself as everyone else's rock, the person countless others leaned on for support and encouragement. Whether it was being my mother's primary caregiver, helping a friend with personal or professional problems, supporting colleagues in cultivating connections with their students, or listening to neighbors who needed encouragement or just a friendly ear ... It was a role I became accustomed to and wore like a badge of honor. This, by no means, meant life was easy, it simply meant that I had the belief that nothing was going to happen to me that God and I couldn't handle together. And I still believe that to this day. However, I now realize that it also served as a shield, actually more of a blockade, to keep me from embracing my own, very real vulnerability. My rock persona enabled me to be that quintessential "pick yourself up by the bootstraps" kind of woman.

I admit that prior to the school assault, I really viewed vulnerability through a very narrow lens. I equated it with, in some ways, a sign of weakness. It was a major disconnect for me to even think that the "rock" and "pick yourself up by the bootstraps" woman could be associated with weakness in any way, shape or form. My identity wouldn't allow me to go there. I wouldn't allow me to go there. If I allowed vulnerability in, how could I continue to be strong for others? What would I do with the primary role I had become accustomed to for so long?

After the school assault, I found myself in a different role, one that was unfamiliar: the role of victim. I recall being home, caught up in a world of physical and emotional pain, trying to make sense out of what happened. My life had gone in a totally unexpected direction, and I was completely out of sorts. I had never met this Eleni before. And I was truly scared when I could not access that "pick yourself up by the bootstraps" woman. What happened to my rock identity? I felt so disconnected, yet I didn't truly realize what was causing the disconnect.

Prior to the school assault, a typical day for me began with getting up at 5:30 AM, heading to school, preparing for classes and being excited about the opportunity to positively impact a student's life. My work was very much a part of my being. After school, I always headed to the gym, as exercise was a normal and important part of my routine. Once home, it was preparing lesson plans, dinner and a little downtime to relax. The weekends were often filled with schoolwork, socializing with dear friends, movies or sporting events.

Now my days were consumed with internal struggles that made it difficult to be future-focused.

I wanted to stop hurting and see a brighter future. Yet, all I could see and feel was the depression and PTSD. And, the assault continued after the initial event. Some students were cyber-bullying me, making threatening comments online. I was so frightened; I couldn't even open the window blinds, imagining there would be someone waiting on the outside to hurt me. On most days, it was difficult to open the door and walk outside or sit in my own yard. I felt like a prisoner in my own home, and I just wanted to not feel fear all the time.

Of course, I was vulnerable (and deep down knew it), but I didn't know how to embrace it. And when you equate vulnerability with weakness, how do you regain your strength? When I didn't see myself as vulnerable, I rarely hesitated when doing most things, and now I hesitated walking out of my own house! I would try to find relief in watching television/movies (thinking the change of focus would help), but the relief never lasted more than a few minutes at a time, and although fleeting, I relished those moments. I found myself on the longest emotional roller coaster ride of my life.

Part of me also felt like I was in a time warp. An hour could seem like an eternity, and yet the days would roll on by quickly, but nothing changed. I did get out of bed each day, sometimes for an hour, sometimes for three or four or more. Although I have to admit that I felt hiding underneath my grandmother's hand-made quilts provided a layer of emotional security and safety. Don't we all seek comfort in the familiar when we're hurting?

I was seeing a lawyer-recommended psychiatrist to deal with the depression and PTSD. He was a kindly, elderly gentleman, and

I felt very safe with him. Leaving my house to drive to those appointments took every ounce of courage I had at the time. In the back of my mind, each time I set foot out the door, I was fearful I would see someone connected to the school assault. Living in an almost constant state of fear can be exhausting and debilitating.

The sessions with my kind and supportive psychiatrist always gave me an emotional booster shot, but the effect didn't last very long. He also prescribed psychotropic drugs recommended for PTSD and situational depression. While I believe he had my best interests at heart, I chose not to take the pharmaceutical route, while absolutely respecting and understanding that it may be the right decision for some people. I had to admit that even though I felt safe with this doctor, I knew I wasn't going to continue moving forward with his methodology. It was time to regain some of my independence, which definitely brought up waves of vulnerability, even though I had yet to embrace it.

I knew in my soul that I was responsible for my healing, and it was time to step up. This, by no means, meant I was going to do it alone. I researched books, articles and interviews on how to deal with PTSD and situational depression. I sought the help of other professionals. I became a student of my own healing. Did everything go as the authorities outlined in their bodies of work? Of course not, but there were some things that did feel right (for me), and I could sense, although quite minor at the time, that I was making forward progress. I was slowly, very slowly, beginning to trust myself again.

Several months after the school assault, a friend invited me out to lunch. Prior to that invitation, I only left the house for doctor's appointments or to get food. At first, I declined, but Beth gently persuaded me. It was the first time I got dressed up and put makeup on, but I was crying underneath.

The old Eleni loved to socialize and dine out with friends, but this was the first time the new Eleni was going out, and I was scared. While I was grateful for my friend's kindness and grace, I couldn't stop the swells of anxiety rising up inside of me, finding myself constantly looking over my shoulder to make sure there was no one there connected to the assault. I finished lunch and went straight home, trying to process why I was so emotional just going out to lunch.

I knew my life was forever changed, but I didn't really know this new Eleni yet. So, how was I to become acquainted with her? I wanted to embrace myself, but admittedly felt stuck. I got very quiet, became introspective, prayed and heard my soul speaking to me. Vulnerability was the answer. Although slowly, I began to accept and embrace vulnerability, realizing that we are all vulnerable. With that awareness came the desire to keep moving forward, regardless of the pace. I was beginning to have grace with myself again.

A few weeks after my lunch out, another friend, who was a videographer and producer, invited me to attend an "Adopt a Pet" day at the Humane Society. Tony knew how much I loved animals and thought it would be good for me to interact with the furry friends and the kind souls who were looking to adopt. I hesitated, really hesitated, questioning whether I had the strength to put on a happy face and connect with others. The irony was that socializing and meeting new people was always one of my favorite things to do. My mother always said I was the quintessential people person and now I hesitated to interact. Tony was encouraging and assured me that he would always be by my side. Deep down, I knew it was time to fully embrace my vulnerability and venture out again. And Tony was right: being around the animals and the wonderful people looking to adopt helped me reconnect to joy (something I hadn't felt in a very long time).

I spent the afternoon playing with animals, talking to people and was even put to work, helping to promote the event. I laughed and smiled. I truly enjoyed engaging and connecting with others. I had a glimpse of the Eleni I knew before, and it felt glorious, like a surprise visit from an old friend. I knew in that moment that I was on the path to "coming back" and was grateful to realize that it wasn't about getting over the fear, but rather moving through it.

Embracing vulnerability is the gateway to accessing your true strengths. You may not be the "rock" in every situation (and you certainly don't have to be), but that in no way means you are not strong.

You don't always have to feel strong in order to be strong.

If you have the courage to face something head-on, you are demonstrating strength and grace. There may be tears, fearful moments, and it doesn't matter. What does matter is that you accept and demonstrate being 100% responsible for your life!

When not embracing vulnerability, you stay in the struggle and embody a victim mentality. Why did this happen to me? How could this have happened? Real growth and progress cannot happen in that space.

It is not that you asked to be hurt or mistreated by someone, nor did you deserve it, but what you do with it is 100% your responsibility.

Do you desire to have a rich and intimate relationship, but have found yourself saying, "I don't want to get hurt," so you don't really go all in? It is one of the real gifts of embracing vulnerability ... yes, you may get hurt, but it is the only path to real intimacy.

You've got to be all in to get to the really good stuff in any area of life!

Own your vulnerability. Own your life.

What would you do if you weren't afraid of getting hurt?

Chapter 3
RENEWAL

"The first step towards getting somewhere is to decide that you are not going to stay where you are."

– J. Pierpont Morgan

RENEWAL

A friend connected me with a catering company that periodically needed to hire additional service staff for events. It was just a few hours, two or three times a month, but as always, I was grateful. I headed home after a day shift, feeling physically tired and yet a bit exhilarated, having been able to work and earn some money. As I turned the corner towards my house, I noticed something strange, but wasn't quite sure what it was. Then I pulled into the driveway, and that little bit of exhilaration quickly left my body.

The foreclosure sign was duct-taped to my front door, for all the world to see. Do the financial institutions want to publicly shame you for no longer being able to pay your mortgage? I was doing everything I could to bring in money, but that doesn't matter to a mortgage company. I had paid my monthly payments on time for a decade, but that didn't seem to matter either. I knew it was time to really reflect on my situation, yet again. My mother always said, "Choose your battles."

I chose to view the foreclosure sign as an invitation from the Universe to get started on my next chapter. I didn't know exactly how that next chapter would unfold, but I did know it wouldn't be in Michigan. Time to begin again.

I decided to move to Florida, where my mother had lived the last thirty-five years of her life. My mother had no retirement and was critically ill for many years before she died. So, I supported her as much as possible, financially and emotionally. I was proud to be of service. She spent countless years taking care of my brothers and me, so why shouldn't she be cared for the same way? As her final gesture of gratitude, my mom willed her condo to me.

Yes, I had a place to go to, and I couldn't have been more grateful. Now, how was I to get there? I didn't have enough money to fill up my gas tank, let alone drive across the country.

I remember walking around my house and looking at all of the wonderful mementoes that held tremendous sentimental value, including many hand-made pieces from my mother and grandmother. And then I looked at the things I had bought, from clothes to furniture to appliances. I could part with those things. I would part with those things. It was time.

I had never hosted my own garage sale and immediately began to feel overwhelmed. Fortunately, dear friends of mine lived around the block and were a tremendous help, guiding me every step of the way. Mike and Jan came over and helped me inventory my possessions and label them with prices. Before I knew it, signs were made advertising the sale, and a few days later, I was open for business. Mike was able to help me each day of the sale, and if he was busy, Jan was ready to fill in. I will always be grateful to them.

I was selling almost everything: clothes, furniture, small appliances, sporting goods, etc. Most of my belongings were moved into the garage, but I was also selling large furniture pieces that remained inside. I'll never forget the first person who was interested in buying my bedroom set. It felt surreal walking her through my home and into the bedroom, as I recalled being excited when I first purchased the set for myself. It's just stuff, I kept telling myself. It's just stuff.

Let it go.

It was a little easier letting go of the smaller items, like clothes ... until my sports' jerseys were put on display. I am a huge sports' fan and will always be loyal to my hometown teams. As I looked at the jerseys on the sale rack, I recalled countless fond memories of my mom taking us to games. Those were great times. *No, not my jerseys*, I thought. *I'm not letting them go*. A customer and I put our hands on a Tigers' jersey at the same time. She asked how much and I said they were no longer for sale. I think I really wanted to feel like I didn't have to give it ALL up. Maybe I felt like I was saying goodbye to the memories too?

The garage sale continued for three days before everything was sold. I made enough money to drive to Florida and support myself for a couple of months.

The journey south began, and I made it all the way to the Sunshine State without incident. I was in the condo for less than a day, trying to reacclimate after the long drive and then decided to head out to purchase supplies (food, cleaning items, etc.), starting to feel good about beginning again.

On my way back from the store, I was

waiting at a red light when I was rear-ended by a distracted driver who was on her phone. My car was hit hard, and I was thrust forward, even though I was wearing a seat belt. I felt like my head and neck snapped.

Before I knew it, I was in an ambulance and back in a neck brace, writhing in pain and screaming ... *are you fucking kidding me? Come on God, I just got here, and I'm ready to start over?* I was so angry. While in the ambulance, I struggled to get up, despite the paramedics' efforts to keep me still. *Why this? Why now? Oh yeah ... I'm vulnerable alright. Now what am I going to do?*

It took some time to calm down, but I knew it was time to step up again. After all, I am 100% responsible for my life.

Even though I was in physical pain, I wanted to find work, knowing the garage sale money wouldn't last very long. But, the pain was winning, and it was extremely difficult to focus on anything else. I had to find a way to keep moving forward and knew dealing with the physical pain had to happen first.

A chiropractor came highly recommended. I began seeing the doctor three times a week for adjustments and started feeling some relief from the pain. BUT I was bored and frustrated. I like to work. I enjoy putting my energy into something to help it grow. Just showing up for an appointment was not enough. During one of my visits, I recall seeing a patient education flyer in the office. From my perspective (as the patient) it was not very inviting or relatable, sensing very few if any patients would actually read it through. So, I was inspired to create a new and improved version. It felt so good to engage my mind again. At my next appointment, I presented the doctor with my creation, and she was pleased. So, I continued to create, and after two weeks the doctor said, "Can I pay you to do this?" Oh, the timing. YES! I was thrilled to hear those words for multiple reasons. I was engaging my mind again, AND the garage sale money had run out. I had already missed two car payments and started to wonder how I could stop my car from being repossessed. I was offered $12 an hour, and my first paycheck was $72. I was so grateful, even though I couldn't make a car payment.

Two weeks into our new agreement, the chiropractor called me. An employee moved on, and they needed someone immediately to work at the front desk, doing data entry and answering phones. $14 an hour, 35 hours per week. The thought of being able to make over $400 a week brought tears to my eyes. I was thrilled. I came in the next day to discuss the position. While the doctor and I were reviewing what my duties and responsibilities were, I was battling an internal struggle. Part of me was trying to be that rock again, that "pick yourself up by the bootstraps" woman, and the other part was fighting back tears because I would soon be losing my car and felt embarrassed. I didn't want to appear scared or worried in front of the doctor. *Thank you, Universe, for giving me another opportunity to embrace my vulnerability. I am vulnerable, and I am still strong.* The doctor sensed I was fighting emotions, so I decided to open up and share my story. She asked me to meet her at a bank later that afternoon. The doctor advanced me two weeks' pay, so I could stop the repo process. I was grateful beyond words.

I reported for work the next day. The fire in my belly was ignited again. I was excited at the thought of being around people on a regular basis and knew that engaging with them would breathe new life into me. Just that awareness made me smile from the inside-out. The Eleni I knew before was coming back, but this time as a new and improved version, ready for the next chapter.

It was definitely on-the-job training, which worked for me, as I was eager to contribute. I quickly settled into the office routine of greeting patients, data entry and answering the phone.

I was raised with a strong work ethic and always believed in doing my job, any job, to the best of my ability. It didn't matter if I was waiting tables, scrubbing toilets or speaking on stage in front of hundreds of people ... I showed up with a positive attitude, always ready and willing to give it my best.

I quickly settled into the routine at the chiropractor's office. After several weeks, I asked my boss if I could be of more service. Again, still very grateful for the work I had, but feeling the tug to contribute even more. I enjoyed problem-solving, creating and being of service and needed to fully engage my mind. The doctor was all in.

I created training protocols and streamlined office processes that improved the overall efficiency of the daily operations. I was still in my data entry position and thrilled to be able to offer more.

Several months had gone by, and I was feeling a regular tug in my soul for something more. I was thrilled to be earning money on a regular basis ($16 an hour at that point) but knew in my heart that this was not my path for the future. My time doing data entry was a bridge, but what was on the other side remained to be seen.

One afternoon an outside consultant hired by the doctor came in to conduct a staff training. It was bittersweet recalling how much I enjoyed the countless teacher trainings I facilitated. I sat quietly, observing the consultant in action. Mary was a friendly person and dressed impeccably, but sorely lacking in leadership and organizational skills. She appeared somewhat confused and kept stopping and restarting the presentation. I could see the frustration on my colleagues' faces, and I found myself growing quite impatient also. While Mary was quite affable, she could not communicate her way out of a paper bag. Now, I don't mind working hard or putting in extra effort, but I do mind wasting time. I clearly recall sitting in that uncomfortable waiting room chair, arms crossed, with a "you've got to be kidding me" look on my face, watching Mary conduct the training. Several times I fought the urge to jump up and take over. While trying to hide my frustration, I couldn't help but think, "One of us is wearing the wrong outfit!" I hear you, Universe ... something has to change.

That evening I had a conversation with a friend I knew from another industry dealing with finance. Richard and I met about fifteen years prior and occasionally collaborated on financial deals together. We worked with small to medium businesses and helped them get money when the banks said no. We were affiliated with private funding groups involved in equipment leasing and accounts receivable financing. While it was very gratifying to help a business owner open their doors, or, in some cases, keep them open, I instinctively helped them holistically, personally and professionally. It was never just about getting them the money. I cared about the whole person and their goals and dreams. I admit, though, that after several years I grew weary of the hoop jumping that some of the funders made business owners go through and left the industry.

When I was sharing with Richard that, even though I was grateful to be earning consistent income, I needed so much more to feed me spiritually, intellectually and financially. He said, "Remember all those times you helped business owners get money for equipment leasing or AR financing, but you instinctively helped them with so many other issues, personal and professional?" "Yes!" I exclaimed. Richard responded, "It's called coaching, and people get paid to do it." What an epiphany! I could go back and do the part of that work that I truly enjoyed.

Richard had left the finance business several years prior. Kendall, his amazing wife, had become a coach and built a hugely successful coach training and certification business with Richard by her side. I knew in that moment I wanted to begin my coaching journey with them.

Kendall was hosting a live event in Dallas the next month, and I jumped at the chance to go. A friend decided to join me. There were over 250 people in attendance (consultants, entrepreneurs, experienced coaches and other curious souls). The $12,000 investment initially kept me from signing up for the coach training/

certification program. After all, at that moment in time, I was earning $16 an hour. The math didn't quite add up.

It really wasn't about the money. It rarely is.

I had to declare to myself, God, and the Universe that I was about to reinvent my life. It was time to truly uplevel. I refused to give myself the option of turning back. As Napoleon Hill references in *Think and Grow Rich*, it was time to burn the ships!

Once you make a declaration like that, things show up that you most likely would have missed otherwise. On Sunday morning, after the conference concluded, I was having breakfast with other conference attendees in the hotel restaurant. A gentleman sitting alone asked me what our group was all about. I told him it was a conference for coaches. We spoke for a few minutes, and he asked if I had a business card. We exchanged information and corresponded periodically. A few months after that initial meeting, he reached out, stating he may need my help as a coach. He was struggling to achieve goals he had previously set for himself. We worked together for six months, and it was an absolute honor to help him get the results he hadn't been able to achieve before. I knew coaching, without question, was more than a big part of my reinvention; it was a calling. I am meant to help people live their best lives, professionally and personally.

While I felt strongly about the work I was doing with the businessman from the conference, deep down, I knew I still hadn't fully stepped into my new identity. The reinvention felt incomplete. I was still working at the chiropractors' office doing data entry and knew in my gut, something had to change. While I appreciated the consistent paycheck, part of me felt like I was holding myself back ... playing it safe, staying in a comfort zone of sorts. We all know real growth happens outside of our comfort zone.

I asked my boss for a private meeting. It was time to step up and really own it, claiming my future. While I was afraid of walking away from the security of a regular paycheck, I was far more fearful of staying the same and not living my best life. When speaking with the doctor, I expressed my sincere gratitude for the opportunity. It was important to me that she know how much I appreciated the lifeline, especially at a time when I needed it the most. I explained that several months earlier, I was contemplating the next chapter and decided to become a business coach, knowing it was the right path for me. She immediately offered to increase my pay and appoint me as her office manager, acknowledging the work I had done to support her clinic and business growth. While I was honored by the offer, I knew it wasn't meant to be a part of my life going forward. I was already far down the path of reinvention. I was a coach. I offered to continue to be of service to the clinic, but this time as a business coach. I would no longer be an employee doing data entry.

Shift happens ... if you allow it. I continued supporting the clinic for a couple of months, and then it was time to move on.

In some ways, you are always in a subtle, but constant state of reinvention, if you are growth-oriented. Phones and software have to get updated periodically, why shouldn't we?

Part of fully embracing reinvention is to also embrace a new identity. At a soul level, I believe we are the same, but as we learn, we grow and evolve. How you presented yourself before the journey began can look quite different from how you present now. When you step into a new identity as part of your reinvention, it forces others around you to change ... or not. Either way, it will impact your relationships. Some people may choose to grow with you, others will not.

I recall sharing my desire to become a coach and start my own business with several people in my circle. Some of the statements I heard were, "But, you've been nothing but a teacher," "You're already in your fifties," and "People don't make real money coaching." While disappointing to hear, I knew those statements were not really about me. They were projecting their limiting beliefs. They saw age and circumstance as obstacles. I saw an opportunity for growth.

Are you holding yourself back because you're letting others rent space in your head?

Be mindful of who you share your goals and dreams with. It is important to be 100% committed to your own growth, regardless of obstacles and circumstance. And always be aware that not everyone in your circle will be on the same path.

Be willing to guard your dreams, like you would anything of real value.

Someone you allowed into your life at one

point may not be a part of your future.

Something you may have done previously is no longer a part of your repertoire. Growth is always a catalyst for change. If you're not growing, you're dying.

Reinvention doesn't mean that something is wrong with you or your life.

Please know, you don't have to be broken to want to be better.

I could have stayed working at the clinic. I was earning enough money to sustain myself, but I wasn't growing the way I wanted to. The choice is always yours'.

I choose growth, even during the difficult times.

What does the
reinvented version
of yourself look like
(inside and out)? Add
specific, quantifiable
details to make your
vision tangible.

Chapter 4
WORTHINESS

"You alone are the judge of your worth and your goal is to discover infinite worth in yourself, no matter what anyone else thinks."

– Deepak Chopra

WORTHINESS

When you actually begin to take stock of honoring yourself, you may be surprised at all the ways you don't. Though you may do it in a big way, there are likely countless small ways where you're not honoring yourself. The two examples I'm about to share may be perceived as small incidents that could be brushed off as insignificant. However, it is in these more intricate moments that I could see all the ways I have not honored myself in the past.

I Never Could Have Done That

It had been a non-stop day at the conference, and I was looking forward to a relaxing dinner and conversation with a fellow attendee. We were both energized by what we had learned and eager to share our personal insights.

We decided to dine at one of the hotel restaurants. The menu offered a variety of options. I chose the portabella mushroom sandwich because the description and associated picture made it look very appealing. The phrase "thick like steak" conjured up a hearty and satisfying meal in my mind. We placed our orders.

We were enjoying an engaging conversation when the food arrived. My dinner companion was having soup and seemed satisfied with her choice. That was not the case for me. I was admittedly disappointed when I looked at my plate. The "thick like steak" portabella mushroom was nowhere to be found. "Thin like paper" was a much more fitting description.

I asked for the waitress to come back to our table. "First, let me say that you've been nothing but kind and attentive and this is no reflection on you." I showed her the sandwich and expressed my disappointment that it was not reflective of the menu description. She picked up my plate, looked at the food and began apologizing profusely. I said I appreciated her concern, reinforcing that it was no reflection on her. She offered to bring me another portabella sandwich. I declined, asking for the menu instead. I ordered another entrée that was far more satisfactory and continued to enjoy the dinner and conversation. A manager was walking around the dining room, checking in on guests. He stopped at our table and inquired about the food and service. I shared my disappointment over the sandwich while reinforcing how considerate the waitress had been. He thanked me for my input. I said, "If it were my house, I would want to know."

As we were preparing to pay for our bills, my dinner companion Linda thanked me for sending my food back. I was admittedly a bit surprised by the comment. When I asked why she was thanking me, Linda stated, "I've been given food that was unsatisfactory before in restaurants, and I never said anything. I ate it and was disappointed in both myself and the food. Thank you for that example of honoring yourself." I was grateful for Linda's words. They reminded me of how I used to feel and of how I have grown and continue to do so. Yes, I have been building a foundation of worthiness.

No Seat Saving

I am a life-long learner and enjoy attending conferences to up my game professionally and personally. The only down-side is having to sit for extended periods each day. Because I am aware of my own physical needs (the herniated discs sustained in the assault make it difficult for me to turn my head often or look at an angle), I make every effort to arrive quite early, so I can choose the most comfortable and appropriate seat when the doors open. This usually meant arriving an hour before the event was to begin. This three-day conference was held in a hotel banquet room with large round tables. There were approximately 150 individuals scheduled to be in attendance.

Before the conference began, the event host announced that there were no assigned seats, and no one was permitted to enter the room prior to the official start time.

On day one of the conference, I arrived at the entrance just over an hour before start time. Two ladies joined me within minutes. We struck up a friendly conversation and decided to sit together. When the doors opened, we walked in and chose a table in the center that would allow me to look straight ahead to the stage. I also chose to sit on the left side of the table because I am right-handed and having the space to write without twisting or turning was far more comfortable. My two new acquaintances and I settled in for a day of learning.

On day two, I was again the first person in line (arriving an hour before the doors were to open) followed quickly by Kim and Debra. We were able to choose a center table again and comfortably enjoy another day of learning and connection.

Day three began as the previous two days had with me, Kim and Debra being the first to arrive. We enjoyed a friendly conversation and were looking forward to another day of learning. The doors opened, and we were the first three people to walk in. As we arrived at the center table, we saw someone's belongings spread over a couple of the chairs, one of them being on the left side where it was most comfortable for me to sit. Kim and Debra took their seats, and I looked around a bit confused. How could these seats already be taken when we were the first people through the door?

Within a couple of minutes, another attendee, named Jeffrey, came to the table and said, "Eleni, you can't sit there. I'm saving that seat for Julie, and she is going to be an hour late." I calmly stated, "Actually Jeffrey, I can sit there, and I am. I was literally the first person to enter the room, and this is the seat I choose." Jeffrey repeated that I couldn't sit there, and I repeated, "I can, and I am." Jeffrey and I went a third round, each of us standing firm. My two new friends told Jeffrey we just wanted to sit together, but rose out of their seats and began to move away. I called them back to the table. I then reminded Jeffrey of the conference rules. No one was allowed to enter before the doors officially opened, nor were you allowed to save seats. "I took the time to arrive an hour early, but I should give up my seat for someone who is going to be an hour late?" That scenario did not make sense to me. After that interaction, Jeffrey removed his belongings, and I took my chosen seat and much to my surprise, Jeffrey stayed seated next to me. I took that gesture as an opportunity to connect on another level.

Kim and Debra said they appreciated me standing up for myself, even though they did not feel comfortable doing so themselves. I could relate to their sentiment, as there were definitely times I simply acquiesced. However, I was grateful for their words, which enabled me to reflect on how I've continued to develop my foundation of worthiness.

You will never regret standing up for yourself. And it doesn't have to be a major, life-altering event. Standing up for yourself in any situation takes courage, and it demonstrates that you believe in your own worthiness. Sending food back or maintaining your seat may seem like trivial acts to some, but each gesture helps to build your foundation of worthiness. By the same token, each time we tolerate something less than what we desire, we erode the foundation.

How many times have you said or thought, "It's OK, I'll just move," or "I'll just eat it, it doesn't matter, it's not that big of a deal"? Could those be excuses to take the path of least resistance and remain firmly ensconced in your comfort zone? Believe me, there was a period of time where I would have just eaten the disappointing food or would have immediately moved to another seat, just because it was easier. Yes, "because it was easier." But it also meant I would have been disappointed in myself and spent the day, as my mother would say, "stewing in my own juices."

I admit I tolerated things that were far less than what I desired. After too many episodes of stewing in my own juices, I knew I had to take a really honest look in the mirror and ask myself a simple question, "Am I not worthy of something better?" Wow. That was quite a wake-up call. I may not have openly verbalized it, but my actions clearly showed that there was a disconnect with worthiness.

I also realized my tolerations extended into other areas of life. I had convinced myself it was "OK" I wasn't earning more money because my work was meaningful. It was "OK" that my significant other wasn't supportive of my professional aspirations, because at least he was honest. How we treat ourselves becomes a guidebook for how others can treat us. If you lower the standards for yourself, how can you expect others to honor you? To celebrate you?

Ask yourself, "Am I being tolerated or celebrated?" A life based on toleration will never be fulfilling. In fact, fulfilment and toleration cannot occupy the same space.

A strong sense of worthiness stems from a core belief of "I am enough." This doesn't mean you don't have to learn, grow and evolve.

But it does mean "I am enough" is the foundation from which to build the life you desire and deserve. Much like a house, a solidly built foundation does not prevent storms from crossing your path, but it does serve to keep you standing.

You do not have to be younger, taller, smarter, more attractive (by whose standards anyway?), etc. You are worthy just as you are.

When you feel worthy at a deep, soulful level, you become the receptacle that allows abundance and love to flow freely to you.

Are you ready to receive?

Step into the Power of You!

What would you
go after if you truly
believed you
deserved it?

Chapter 5
ABUNDANCE

"Abundance is not something we acquire. It is something we tune into."

– Dr. Wayne Dyer

ABUNDANCE

Investing in Yourself

It was the last day of the coaching event in Dallas, which also meant it was the last chance to sign up for the certification program at the special conference rate. I knew I wanted to be a professional coach. I knew I wanted to study with Kendall. However, there were some things I did not know. How was I going to pay the $12,000 investment for training and certification? How could I even use my credit card with a current limit of only $3,000? At that point in time, I was earning $16 per hour doing data entry at the chiropractic clinic and was very grateful for the steady income, but couldn't make the leap, in my mind, to investing $12,000.

I was sitting at a table in the back of the conference center. Kendall asked, "On a scale of one to ten, how committed are you to becoming a coach?" I shouted out "Twelve!" from the back of the room. Kendall heard and called me out.

"Eleni, have you signed up yet?" I shrunk down in my seat and wished I had kept my mouth shut. Somehow, I found the strength to respond. "No, but I'm going to." Again, why couldn't I just keep my mouth shut? OK, now I had to do something.

I stepped outside of the conference room. While walking back and forth in the lobby, I kept running the numbers through my head. *I make $16 an hour, and my current credit limit is $3,000. How was I supposed to invest $12,000?* What the hell was I thinking? Why even consider such a thing? How could I invest $12,000 when I had nothing in the bank? I couldn't outrun those thoughts in my mind.

And then I thought about the previous night. Kendall had invited several of her clients on stage to share their success stories. I was sitting next to my friend (and conference roommate) Cynthia. Just as the first panelist began speaking, Cynthia said she wasn't feeling well and headed back to the room. I remained in the audience and listened intently as each coach shared her journey to success. I found myself feeling inspired and excited about what was possible for me. Before I left the venue, I approached one of the panelists and asked if I could speak with her sometime soon, as I wanted to hear more of her story.

Later on, when I arrived back at the hotel room, I found Cynthia pacing back and forth and stating in an angry tone, "We are not like them," over and over. I said, "First, cut out the 'we' shit. And second, what are you talking about?" She asked, "What is wrong with making $5,000 a month?" I replied, "Not a damn thing if that is what you need, and that makes you happy." Cynthia started talking about the success panel and went back to repeating, "We are not like them." I stopped her and said, "Cynthia, it is you and I that are not alike. When the success panel came on stage, you ran away. I stayed and went up to them, asking questions, wanting to know more."

Thinking of that exchange with Cynthia really made me reflect, and I'm grateful. I could have gone home and lived a "pleasant" life, one that most likely would not have been nearly as rewarding financially, intellectually or spiritually.

So, I asked myself, *What will my life look like if I don't move forward with this?*

That question triggered something in me. Why even consider this? Because it is my future. I reminded myself that remaining at the chiropractic clinic long-term was not the future that was going to feed my soul. I needed to feel more fulfilled while still being of service to others. Yes, my desire to be a coach was a 12 on a scale of 1-10.

Now it was time to figure it out. I drew upon the old cliché, "Where there's a will, there's a way." I called the credit card company to ask for a limit increase. I told them I was starting a business and needed to invest the money in my own training. They asked a few questions about the business and reviewed my payment history. Gratefully, the data entry job allowed me to now make regular payments on time. After two minutes on hold (which seemed a lot longer while I was pacing back and forth in the lobby), the agent informed me that my limit was being increased to $13,000. What? I was surprised, grateful and anxious, all at the same time. No more excuses!

I marched back into the conference, credit card in hand and headed to the registration area and turned right around inches away from the table. I didn't even break stride. My mind went right back to "What the hell am I doing charging

$12,000 when I only make $16 an hour?" I took a few deep breaths and reminded myself about the future I desired. I walked back up to the table, this time letting the team member touch the card, but, not even the jaws of life could have pried it out of my hands. I again retreated. I was walking in circles and rocking back and forth as the anxiety rose inside of me.

I started asking myself questions to confront the shit going on inside my mind.

Am I saying I can't do this? Am I saying I don't have the ability to make this work? Am I willing to kiss away my future plans? Oh, hell no! Saying yes to any of those questions wasn't acceptable in any way. A yes response would have meant I wasn't worthy of the investment or worthy of a brighter future. I walked right back up to the registration desk, released my credit card and filled out the form. Admittedly, the anxiety was still riding high, and I actually threw up in my mouth (not one of my proudest moments), but I remained standing. I was on my way to becoming a certified professional business coach.

The fear I felt when the opportunity to become a coach appeared made me realize I had very limiting beliefs about abundance and was stuck in a scarcity mindset. I was so hesitant to invest the $12,000 because at a core level I believed I might never see the money return to me, and that was frightening. My mind was entirely focused on what would be missing from my bank account, not what could come my way.

Knowing how to acquire money helps release limiting beliefs that can put a huge "kink in the hose" (meaning things will not flow freely to you or from you, blocking access to the abundance in the Universe).

There is ample money in the Universe, and it is meant to be in circulation.

How could I be ready and willing to receive, if I'm also not willing to put something out into the Universe? But shit, it was $12,000 on a $16 an hour pay scale. I was scared. It was a full-on tug-of-war.

The Law of Polarity states that everything has an opposite...its equal and opposite. Everything is created as a whole (right/left, top/bottom, up/down, etc.). You cannot have just one side of an object or situation. The opposite side must also exist, and it exists in the same space. We would not have positive without the negative or day without night. The opposite of acceptance is resistance. Where you choose to focus your energy and attention determines which side of the spectrum you experience. Yes, I was creating $12,000 of debt by investing in the training, but, that also meant that the money and the means to earn it also existed (even if I couldn't clearly see it yet).

We live in an abundant Universe, but admittedly I didn't always feel that way (especially after the school assault and losing my house). And, limiting beliefs will block you from receiving the gifts of abundance. A scarcity mindset keeps the focus on what is missing, creating that proverbial kink in the hose. If you are focused on problems, your mind is sure to find more problems, and you end up missing out on opportunities. When you believe in abundance, you are training your mind to look for opportunities. You will see solutions that were not visible to you before, yet they absolutely always existed. Remember, the Law of Polarity shows us that everything is created as a whole.

Build your "resilience muscle," especially during difficult times, by understanding that a solution (even when not readily visible) does exist.

Believing what you need already exists is the first step to receiving. You must also accept 100% responsibility for your life. When you step into your power, you put yourself in the driver's seat. Yes, the money, opportunities and abundance you desire exist, but it is vital that you are fully aware of what will cause those things to come into your life. Be proactive.

The Law of Cause and Effect states that every cause has its effect and every effect has its cause. All actions have a corresponding reaction. Understanding that we are the first cause, and energy returns to its source, gives you the power to create more abundance in your life.

Are you aware of how much power lies within you? You can literally cause amazing results to positively impact you and your environment.

Initially, at the registration table, I only saw that I was creating an additional debt of $12,000. I didn't view it as an investment and couldn't get past how or when I was going to earn the money back. That train of thought fueled my limiting beliefs and kept me stuck in a scarcity mindset. I was giving my power away, which was a direct path to living with an abundance of lack. I was not behaving as if I was 100% responsible and in control of my life. And our behaviors are always reflective of our beliefs.

So, I looked at my beliefs regarding my own worthiness, giving myself a reality check. Did I have a scarcity mindset regarding my own abilities? It was a tough question to ask, but it was the kick in the ass I needed. Hell yes, I was worthy of a bright future. Hell yes, I have the skills and experience to get me there. I was definitely worthy of a $12,000 investment and so much more. Stepping into my power was liberating. I could create the life I desired. I began to embrace that I am truly the cause that creates the effects (results and circumstances) that exist in my life.

I felt an awakening happening inside of me, connecting to the energy of abundance.

As Dr. Wayne Dyer so eloquently stated,

"Abundance is not something we acquire. It is something we tune into."

My mind was now open to possibilities. I was tuning into the abundance of the Universe and accepting full responsibility for my life.

I was able to pay off that credit card debt within eight months.

When you are energetically aligned with abundance, the opportunities will present themselves. However, you must still be the cause that brings in the desired effects. Take consistent action aligned with what you truly desire.

While I have met many clients organically, I still had to take action. Regardless of whether the first encounter occurred at an airport, restaurant or business event, I initiated conversation and cultivated the relationships.

I believed there were clients I was meant to serve (even if I didn't know exactly where) and I understood cause and effect. My beliefs and understanding helped to propel me forward.

Yes, we do live in an abundant Universe, but as Wayne Dyer stated, "It is something we tune into."

Scarcity Mindset

There's never enough!
Sound familiar?
Whether you're talking about money, food,

clients or anything else, the belief that there is never going to be enough will cause your thoughts and actions to be representative of lack.

I was at a business networking function that was attended by over 100 professionals in various industries. I've always had an outgoing and friendly personality and enjoy meeting people and hearing their stories. Now, I'm not completely naïve, and I realize many people attend these events solely to find a client on the spot.

I was engaged in a lively conversation with a fellow attendee who was very curious about my philosophy on coaching, as he was considering hiring someone to help him reach his business goals. Of course, I was happy to share. Several minutes into our discussion, a man (who also happened to be a professional coach) came running over and stepped in between us, stating, "I spoke with him first! He's mine." Were we on an elementary school playground? Did I take the last toy? He was actually laying claim that the gentleman I was speaking with was already his client. The gentleman immediately responded, "I never said I wanted to engage

MY REVINVENTED LIFE

your services and now, rest assured, it will not happen."

The other coach was exhibiting a strong scarcity mindset. Even though I didn't have the chance to ask him directly, I'll bet he absolutely thought that there were not enough clients in the world for each of us. A scarcity mindset can act as a repellent to abundance, and you will miss opportunities. Because I learned to embrace abundance, I believe there are more than enough clients for each of us. I also choose to view someone else's success as a demonstration of what is possible. Then I work at being the cause to bring it into my own life. You still have to do the work!

Abundance of Lack

I was speaking before a group of bankers and entrepreneurs, discussing people's relationship with money. The presentation included mindset, universal laws and abundance. A woman approached me after my talk and said, "You say we live in an abundant Universe and that there is enough money to go around. Then why do I have so many bills to pay and so much

98

debt?" I said, "It is all abundance, but right now you have an *abundance of lack*." I honestly was not trying to be a smart ass. I wanted to get her attention to further the discussion, knowing that all she could currently see was lack, no doubt stemming from her belief in scarcity. Again, where you choose to focus your thoughts is training your mind. Focus on lack, and your mind will continue to find lack. Much to her credit, she was open to further dialogue.

A lack mentality brought on by a scarcity mindset can also cause people to look for a quick fix, a bandage to stop the bleed. You cannot grow anything sustainable in that headspace. And, you are not setting yourself up to be the receptacle, ready to receive your desired abundance. Remember the Law of Cause and Effect? It is important to be proactive, not reactive. To tap into the abundance of the Universe, start with the belief that you are already enough, just as you are. Of course, you will learn and grow, but at a soulful level, you already are enough. Believe that what you desire exists and ask yourself how strong the desire is. Do you really, *really* want it?

Napoleon Hill stated, "The starting point of all achievement is **desire**. Keep this constantly in mind. Weak **desires** bring weak results, just as a small fire makes a small amount of heat."

Keep focused on what is possible.

You can learn how to create more abundance in your life, to be the cause that brings it in. Believe you are your own foundation to attract and build more.

Stop putting the kink in the hose.

You are made for more!

In what three areas
of your life can you
tune into your current
abundance?

Chapter 6
GRATITUDE

*"Acknowledging the good
you already have in your
life is the foundation for all
abundance."*

– Eckhart Tolle

GRATITUDE

Gratitude and resentment cannot live in the same place. Where are you choosing to live?

Clearwater Beach is consistently rated as one of the nicest beaches in the nation. So, it is no surprise that it would be crazy busy on a sunny Saturday. I actually live on a peninsula between the city and the beach. One way on, one way off. Driving on the causeway bridge is a normal part of my day. But this day was a little more interesting.

I found myself laughing when I recalled saying, "I'm so grateful for this traffic." "I'm so grateful for the crowds of people causing such a slowdown." "I'm grateful that I'm not driving on snow and ice" (not something that a Florida resident worries about anyway).

I was returning home from the gym Saturday morning and could see the traffic backed up as I approached the bridge. Once on the bridge, my car started to choke and then stall. Now, the traffic was literally bumper to bumper, so my options were limited, and I was on a bridge, so where was I to go? I immediately felt anxious, wondering what the hell I was going to do. I put the car back in park, and it started again. Thank God! The relief was short-lived. A minute later, my car choked and stalled again. I put it back in park and was able to start again. That cycle repeated six times, and I grew more anxious and nervous with each one. What was I supposed to do, stuck in the middle of this traffic with a dying car? I had to find a way to basically get a grip and calm myself, as I was on the verge of a real meltdown.

My mind immediately shifted to gratitude. I knew I had to find something to be grateful for, even in this situation. "I'm so grateful for this traffic." "I'm so grateful that people are moving so slow because they won't rear-end me." "I'm so grateful that I'm not driving on snow and ice." I kept repeating those statements, and my breathing became less labored, and I could feel my heart rate coming back to normal.

I made it safely off the bridge and onto the peninsula. Fortunately, there is a gas station with a full-service mechanic close by. I choked, stalled and restarted my way onto their parking lot. The mechanic said it would be over an hour before he would have a chance to check out the problem. I left the car there and walked the two blocks home, still feeling grateful that I was not hurt and did not cause an accident.

I had no idea what the problem was with my car. So, I had no idea what it would cost to get fixed. What I did know at that moment in time was that the only food I had was three cans of beans in the pantry, and I had $11 dollars to my name. No, I did not forget any zeros or decimal points. I also knew that whatever was wrong with my car would require a lot more than $11. And yet, I was able to stay in the energy of gratitude and remained calm and even cheerful. I was dancing around my condo, giving thanks for all that I had. "I'm so grateful I have a safe place to live." "I'm so grateful I am physically able to walk." "I am so grateful for my faith and spirit." And the list went on.

The mechanic called a couple of hours later to inform me about the issues with my car and stated that repairs would cost just over $700. I told him to go ahead and make the repairs. In that moment I had no idea where I was going to get the money to pay the bill. I had $11 and three cans of beans, and I expressed gratitude for it all. I wouldn't allow myself to focus on what I didn't have in the bank or the pantry.

I had already started my coaching business, but admittedly I had fallen into a bit of a slump. I had no current clients at that time. When you focus on lack, I believe you attract more of the same. How much do you enjoy being around people who only talk about what is wrong or what they don't have? I knew the importance of keeping my energy focused on gratitude. "I'm grateful to be able to help people." "I'm grateful that I believe in connection and cultivating relationships." "I'm grateful to be a woman of faith." "I'm grateful for my health."

Within seven days of my car dying on the bridge, I had signed on two new clients who paid in full for their coaching programs. I went from $11 to $22,500 in one week. I believe, with every fiber of my being, that I would not have attracted those clients if I wasn't in a constant state of gratitude. Being grateful for what currently exists in your life is the conduit to attract even more.

And, you must be all in with gratitude. You cannot be a fair-weather fan. You're either living a life of gratitude or you're not. Like any relationship, it is not 50-50. It must be 100-100. Is every day completely good? No. Is there some good in every day? Yes. Let's say you have ten events happen during your day: nine are successful, but one doesn't go well. What do most people choose to focus on? Be mindful.

Living a life of gratitude doesn't mean you should be grateful if something goes wrong or that you deserved to be hurt. But, you can be grateful that you had the strength to deal with it. You can be grateful for any insights or lessons learned that could help you moving forward.

If you focus on the struggle, you stay in the struggle and resentment soon follows. And, I understand, first-hand, the slippery slope of resentment when you feel you've been "done wrong." *Why me? Why did this happen to me? It isn't fair.* Resentment is like a brick wall that will keep you stuck! Keep your focus on the injustice of a situation, and you will keep adding bricks to that wall.

If you focus on the lessons in the situation and can be grateful for what you do have, you're giving yourself a valuable gift. You have taken your power back and are moving from victim to victor!

Learning to be grateful, even when it is difficult and painful is the only way to move forward.

Gratitude and resentment cannot live in the same space.

Where are you choosing to live?

What are you most
grateful for?
(Don't forget to put
yourself on the list!)

Chapter 7
BOUNDARIES

"Whatever you are willing to put up with is exactly what you will have."

– Anonymous

BOUNDARIES

Why are the double yellow lines painted down the center of roads?

Why do dog owners have fences around their backyards?

Why is there a backstop behind home plate?

These are all examples of concrete physical boundaries that are meant to keep us safe from harm. Boundaries that cannot be seen or touched are just as vital, if not more so, to our safety and general wellbeing. Maintaining boundaries is an essential part of self-care. Invisible boundaries are an important component of all relationships, personal and professional, and should be beneficial to everyone involved.

My business coaching practice was growing, and I was thrilled to be developing a strong, local client base. As any business owner knows, the best compliment is when a satisfied client refers someone to you. Two of my local clients suggested I connect with Colette, a massage therapist, who was also versed in the healing arts. Colette and I were already acquainted, as we shared several friends in common and spoke at many social gatherings. We scheduled a time to meet to discuss her business goals. Up to this point, she only worked intermittently with massage clients and was ready to step up and into her power as a business owner. Colette was excited to turn her passion for massage and the healing arts into a profitable business, and I was honored to help her create a vision for the future. I shared a proposal outlining what we had discussed and what would be involved in our work together. Colette immediately said she wanted to hire me. I presented the investment, and she said yes, without hesitation, signing the contract. We chose a starting date and Colette agreed to pay the deposit at least 48 hours in advance of our first session, as stipulated in the contract.

Prior to the beginning of our professional engagement, we connected in our common social circles, cultivating a friendship. During many of our conversations, Colette often commented that she was grateful to be moving forward with her business vision. I reinforced that it was my honor to help her vision become reality. The start date drew near. The 48-hour mark passed, and I had not received the deposit. I called Colette and she stated she wasn't ready to begin. I inquired why and her response was not what I expected. She said, "We have become friends. You should just give this to me. Friends shouldn't charge each other." I responded, "You specifically stated you wanted to 'hire' me. It is my business, my livelihood, to help people develop their own profitable and rewarding business." She became even more adamant that I should "just give this to her." I then asked if it would be OK if I came over for three massages every week, at no charge, of course. Colette said that would be ridiculous and she would never allow such a thing. But, I should give away my professional services? I suggested we agree to disagree and moved on.

Could I have given away my services? Yes. Would I have felt good about it? No. It would have ended up eroding the relationship, even if Colette was initially happy and sessions were productive. I have no doubt resentment would have grown inside of me and, let's be honest, our time together would have not been pleasant.

You cannot build a sustainable relationship (personally or professionally) with things out of balance. I've never been a fan of the phrase, "Relationships are 50-50." I believe they should be "100-100," where everyone involved is committed to the success of the relationship. A key component of that success is respect, for each other and what is brought to the table. Yes, there is give and take, but there needs to be balance. One person cannot always be the giver or taker. Healthy boundaries help to maintain that balance.

For those of us who are self-proclaimed innate nurturers, it is almost a calling to be there for someone in need. We go on autopilot. Now, I absolutely believe in being of service and lending a helping hand. However, there was a long period when it was often at the expense of my own time, energy or financial stability. I was becoming too drained to properly care for myself. Once you are on that slippery slope, it is only a matter of time before you are unable to help anyone, including yourself.

We nurturers can create enabling relationships and struggle to create boundaries. Outwardly you may always appear compassionate, supportive and kind. Yet, inwardly you could harbor anger and resentment because you feel like you've been taken advantage of and you're not getting the respect you deserve. My wake-up call was realizing I was not respecting myself, which was an important lesson to learn. Even though it can be challenging, creating boundaries is meant to empower everyone involved. And, I say this as a recovering enabler ... it is important to give someone the chance to step into their own power!

Today is April 4th, 2020. Isn't it amazing how quickly life can change? I began writing this chapter just over a month ago before the coronavirus became a global pandemic. With each passing day, the number of cases increases, and the subsequent ripple effect has touched us all. "Safer at home," "social distancing" and "quarantined" are now commonly used terms that are a part of everyone's vocabulary. And, they are all examples of physical boundaries, designed to keep us safe.

I have been adhering to the suggested guidelines and spending my time at home. Now, I'm quite a gregarious individual, so adapting to social distancing requires a considerable conscious effort. I remind myself that these physical boundaries are designed to keep us safe.

But, what about the boundaries you can't see?

We are in a collective crisis, and when in crisis mode, we must respond, and respond quickly. Like many people, I immediately began doing outreach to family, friends and clients to see if I could be of service. I offered to help anyone that asked. I feel it is a privilege to be of service and consider it an honor when others trust me by reaching out for help in their time of need. I was helping entrepreneurs pivot to sustain their businesses, presenting Master Classes to organizations to help them navigate through these challenging times and tending to an elderly neighbor. I went on autopilot in full caretaker mode. Whenever anyone reached out, I said yes.

Just a couple of days ago, I was having a conversation with a dear friend, and she happened to ask, "How is your book coming along?" Wait, what? My book?

Was I working on my book? No. Was I taking

good care of myself? No. Was I focusing on my own business? No. Was I starting to get annoyed with myself? Yes.

That simple question from my friend was the kick in the ass I needed to be reminded about the importance of boundaries, especially those that are invisible. We all need boundaries to survive, let alone thrive. Again, I am absolutely honored to be able to lift a spirit, lend a helping hand and empower others, especially during times like these. However, it soon became apparent that I had gone down that slippery slope again. Continuing to serve without properly caring for myself would soon mean there was nothing left in the tank to give.

When I realized the invisible boundaries had been crossed, my solution wasn't to go into complete self-preservation. That is simply not in my nature. My solution was to find balance.

Yes, I want to keep being of service and I will. It is absolutely my passion and mission to empower others. But, if I had continued putting myself on the back burner, how much longer would I be able to help others? Self-care is vital, now more than ever. Let's remember to refill our own tanks.

If you are struggling to create those invisible boundaries or think they are not always necessary ... imagine what would happen if those lines on the road faded or were moved to one side. What if the backstop was removed from the baseball game? What if yards with dogs had no fences?

"No" is a complete sentence.

If someone reaches out for support and it is not an urgent matter that needs to be dealt with immediately, I schedule it into my calendar. Please hear me, it is OK to say no. You can even practice saying no in different ways. "I'm not available for that." "It is not a fit for me." "That is not going to work for me." Do not apologize or make excuses. "No" is a complete sentence. Just like your bank account, if you allow continuous withdrawals (without making deposits) you end up drained and depleted, unable to help anyone else (including yourself).

I have learned to put my own needs (sleep, exercise, business, working on my book, etc.) into the calendar, as it serves to help me maintain boundaries. I am taking better care of myself, so I can care for others.

Boundaries. They are meant to keep us safe while still allowing us to serve. Healthy boundaries are empowering for all involved.

My heart and infinite respect go out to first responders, doctors, nurses, mail carriers, delivery people and grocery store employees who continue to serve, even without all necessary boundaries to support all of us.

Who do you need to
set boundaries with?

Chapter 8
TIMELESSNESS

*"Laughter is timeless.
Imagination has no age.
Dreams are forever."*
– Walt Disney

TIMELESSNESS

"You're already in your fifties. Why start something new? Why don't you just retire?" When I spoke of my goals and vision for the future, I was often met with "But, you're already in your fifties." Now, I am well aware, for some people, being north of fifty makes them feel old. I am not one of them. I am sixty years old as I write this, and in many ways, I am just getting started! Be mindful of who you share your dreams with and know that their projections are connected to their limiting beliefs, not you!

You are most likely familiar with the phrase, "You're past your prime." I believe you and only you decide what your "prime" is and how and when it plays out.

How old is too old to do something new? For me, so long as I have the desire, it is never too late!

Attitude trumps age every day of the week! I turned sixty last year and greeted the new decade with open arms. Why shouldn't I?

Countless people have said, "Wow, you don't look your age." Now, I absolutely believe they meant that statement as a compliment, but why shouldn't sixty look good, or any other number for that matter? An individual's spirit and energy are so much more than the birthdate on their driver's license.

I went to Las Vegas with a dear friend to celebrate my sixtieth, with plans to see shows each night. One evening, I went to see Mat Franco, a very talented magician who won *America's Got Talent*. I heard great things about his show and was excited to be in the audience. Like many magicians, Mat asked for volunteers from the audience to come up on stage. Needless to say, I was just thrilled to be chosen, along with two other people. He had us standing in three different spots on stage, and one by one approached us, asking our names, where we were from and what brought us to Las Vegas.

When Mat walked up to me with the microphone, I said, "My name is Eleni. I'm from Detroit, and I'm here celebrating my sixtieth birthday." He said, "Great, thanks," and began walking to the next person, then stopped in his tracks. Mat immediately turned around, looked at me and said, "Sixty, damn, good for you!" I smiled and thanked him. While mingling in the lobby after the show, several people came up to me to wish me a happy birthday and tell me that they thought I was much younger. I graciously thanked them. I would never take a sincere compliment for granted.

I must give credit where credit is due! My mother always had the best attitude regarding age and would never hesitate to share her number. I recall a friend asking her why she was always so willing to state her age. My mother replied, "I'm so damn proud I made it through another year, why wouldn't I shout it from the mountain tops?" Lula had a great sense of humor, an amazing spirit, and was a life-long learner, constantly wanting to engage her mind to grow. She was an avid reader who loved studying something new on a regular basis. Lula's thirst for knowledge kept her intellectually curious and active (even when her body could not).

My mother never let age stop her from dreaming and believing in the future. Her spirit was undeniable. Now, none of us can stop the clock from ticking, but we do have total control over our beliefs and thoughts as time marches on. I will be eternally grateful that I was taught to be future-focused, regardless of my age. I fondly recall Lula often saying, "Every day you wake up is a chance for a dream to come true." Thank you, Mom, for your amazing spirit!

I was fifty-four years young when those internal nudges for change kept crossing my mind. Working in the chiropractic clinic did give me some fulfilment and regular income, but I desired and needed more. When I envisioned my future, years down the road, I didn't see myself there. I feared waking up years later, only to realize that I had let go of my dreams. Time to act!

Yes, I started my own business in my mid-fifties. Yes, I was excited (and still am) about the future. Yes, I wanted to be of service and help others live their best lives. My passion led me to coaching. I am honored to help entrepreneurs and executives overcome money and mindset blocks, so they can create the income, impact and lifestyle they desire.

None of us is meant to do this alone. We all need someone to guide and encourage us to reach our full potential. I am humbled and grateful to be able to be that person for others. When I first met Adam, he was a corporate executive in his mid-fifties. He loved his actual work, but, in his words, had grown tired of the corporate scene. Adam said he was afraid of waking up at sixty-five and realizing he had wasted one of his best decades. We began working together. I helped him create his own consulting business, so he could leave his corporate job. Adam stated, "You gave me my life back. I am once again fired up about my future." I want you to be fired up about your future too.

And yes, there are many people who began a completely new chapter later in life. The following are just a few examples of individuals (I know there are countless others) who did not allow age to inhibit their goals and dreams. It would be impossible to measure the number of lives that have been positively influenced as a result of their work. I am grateful to those brave souls who do not let age deter them from moving forward. You are all shining examples of "attitude trumps age," and your legacies live on!

Betty White

Betty has enjoyed the longest television career of any entertainer, spanning 80 years – age **98**. She won her first Emmy at age **53** and her most recent at age **88**.

Louise Hay

Louise opened her own publishing company, Hay House, at age **61** and became a New York Times bestselling author at age **62**. Louise also released her first film at age **82**.

Harland David Sanders

Harland opened Sanders' Café in Corbin, Kentucky at age **49** and began the Kentucky Fried Chicken franchise at age **65**.

Duncan Hines

Duncan wrote his first food and hotel guide at age **55** and licensed the right to use his name to the company that developed Duncan Hines' cake mixes at age **73**.

Laura Ingalls Wilder

Laura published the first book in her Little House on the Prairie series at age **65**.

Anna Mary Robertson Moses (Grandma Moses)

Grandma Moses began painting at age **78**. Hallmark purchased the rights to use her paintings on greeting cards and some of her work appears in the Smithsonian American Art Museum.

Frank McCourt

Frank wrote the Pulitzer Prize-winning Angela's Ashes at age **66**.

Jerry Saltz

Jerry was a long-distance truck driver until the age of **41**, before becoming an art critic. He became the senior art critic for New York magazine at age **55** and won the Pulitzer Prize for Criticism at age **67**.

Ernestine Shepherd

Ernestine started body building at **56**, became competitive and was twice declared the world's oldest female body builder by Guinness World Records in 2010 and 2016. Ernestine has continued her body building lifestyle into her **80s**.

Susan Boyle

Susan was **47** years old when she auditioned for Britain's Got Talent, impressing judges and the audience singing "I Dreamed A Dream" and soon became a global sensation.

As I'm writing this chapter, I am in quarantine due to COVID-19, as are countless others. So, I decided to look after my ninety-six-year-old neighbor, Bob, doing my best to keep him safe from the pandemic.

Bob and I met a few years ago, and even though we both happen to be from the same town in Michigan, we had no prior connection before meeting in Florida. We soon discovered that Bob and my mother went to high school together and graduated the same year. Cue "It's a small world after all."

Bob and I spoke several times a day, discussing everything from world events to sports, entertainment and family. A close friendship arose through those daily conversations, and I realized early on that the spirit of timelessness was alive and well in my neighbor. He, too, was a life-long learner. I recall one of our visits when I heard Spanish being spoken in the background. Bob was listening to one of his audio lessons. Learning a new language at ninety-six years of age is truly timeless.

Marian was another neighbor of mine. I fondly recall the day we met in the lobby six years ago. She was impeccably dressed, with her hair done up and wearing bright red lipstick. I told her how pretty she looked and asked where she was going "all gussied up." Marian replied, "It's my ninety-third birthday, and some friends are taking me out for lunch." I said, "My birthday was just last week." We became fast friends and dined together every month. Our conversations were always engaging. There was no sign of an age gap.

Marian was also very active socially and several times a week got dressed up, put makeup on and treated herself to dinner, always with the perfect martini. She had a true zest for life, finding something to look forward to and enjoy each day.

During one of our evenings out, I asked Marian if she always had this "live life to the fullest" attitude. Her response surprised me. "I was always quite anxious, quite the worry-wort and didn't really enjoy life as much as I could have." I asked what changed. Marian told me that her husband of over fifty years died when she was seventy-nine, and that was her wake up call. She said, "When my husband died, I realized that so much in life isn't worth worrying about, and I didn't want to start a new decade feeling miserable."

Marian didn't let age or circumstance stop her. Marian was ninety-nine-years-old when she passed away last year. She gave herself the gift of twenty fulfilling years. Timeless!

What are you missing out on or denying yourself, by not being future-focused?

It ain't over 'til it's over!!

What would you do if you didn't think about your age?

Chapter 9
FORGIVENESS

"There is no love without forgiveness, and there is no forgiveness without love."

– Bryant H. McGill

FORGIVENESS

Forgiveness is ultimately a tool of freedom. It is a gift you give yourself.

I didn't always feel that way.

I was thinking back to a time when I came home from school one day, very upset over something a friend had done. Our second-grade class was performing several vignettes in connection with our current social studies lesson. Mrs. Balloid chose six group leaders who were to select their cohorts for the individually assigned vignette. I was so excited when my friend Laura asked me to be in her group. We rehearsed for two days and were to perform on the third. I came to class with a big smile on my face, looking forward to participating in our little play. When I walked over to our group, Laura approached me and said I was no longer included. Another student, who was absent the day groups were chosen had come back, and Laura wanted her to take my place. I felt so sad and hurt.

The walk home seemed a lot longer that day for this eight-year-old. I told my mother with tears in my eyes how hurt I was. In that moment, I couldn't imagine not being angry at Laura. Of course, my mom listened, offered support and helped me to calm down.

She and my grandmother then shared their wisdom on the importance of forgiveness. I remember snapping back, "But Laura hurt me. Why should I forgive her? She's the one who did something wrong." My mom said forgiving Laura does not excuse her behavior, but it would help me stop being so angry.

Little did I know at that time that I would be given ample opportunity to learn that lesson.

I recall a time when I discovered a significant other had cheated. We had been dating for several months, agreed to be exclusive and saw each other three to four times a week. Victor never hesitated to share his feelings and tell me how happy he was. We also often spent time with his family, including his parents, engaged in heartfelt conversation, each time we were at their home. In fact, his parents would occasionally call me just to chat. I felt our relationship growing closer (or so I thought).

During one of our visits, Victor's parents were talking about their upcoming fortieth wedding anniversary and the desire to celebrate in a special way. So, Victor and I decided to plan a party to be held at their favorite restaurant. The gathering was to include immediate family, a few close friends and myself. I was looking forward to being a part of the festivities.

I never made it to the anniversary party.

A week before the party, Victor and I were headed out to dinner, when I noticed an ID badge and lipstick in his car that obviously belonged to another woman. When I asked about those things, Victor said he just gave a ride home to a colleague. Although it sounded plausible, it just didn't feel right in my gut.

A few days later, I had to drop something off at his parents' house. When I walked in, I found Victor's father sitting alone at the kitchen table with a sad look on his face. I asked if something was wrong and could see him getting emotional. Victor had confessed to him that he had started seeing the new colleague at work, and he felt I had a right to know. My gut already knew. I cried and thanked him for caring about me. I then apologized because I could no longer attend their anniversary party. As much as I wanted to be there for them, it would have been too awkward and painful. Victor's father was very gracious and said he completely understood.

About a week after the party, Victor started calling again and leaving messages. He apologized over and over, said he made a mistake, begged for forgiveness and asked if we could get back together. I didn't answer those messages. I was hurt, angry and spent many a night crying into my pillow. I wasn't thinking about the next week or month and just wanted to get through a day feeling good again.

A couple more weeks went by, and my hurt and anger were still dominating my thoughts and energy. Then the light bulb moment hit me right between the eyes. I wasn't the one who cheated, but I was the one still suffering. I had entered a self-imposed emotional prison, but I knew the way out!

My mother's voice again echoed in my mind. "Forgiveness will help you stop being angry."

I reached back out to Victor and scheduled a time to meet with him in person. He again apologized profusely and asked to be forgiven. A sense of calm came over me, and I said, "I absolutely do forgive you, Victor." There was peace in my heart as the words came out of my mouth. Victor responded, "I'm so glad, now we can get back together." I said no. "I am forgiving you to set myself free, not to get back with you." Forgiving him really helped me come back to myself.

Yes, I know pain and heartache, as do you. After the school assault, there was a long period of time when I was so caught up in the anger and fear that I could barely think. My mind was completely consumed by the physical pain and subsequent betrayal. I was stuck on an emotional runaway train with no end in sight. *How could they hurt me that way? Why would they betray me? Why me?* I felt powerless, like I had lost control over my own thoughts.

If you cannot think freely for yourself, how are you to live an empowered life? How are you to move forward? I found myself trapped in an emotional prison. The individuals connected to the assault still had power over me. They moved on with their lives. I did not. I could not let go of what they did to me. It was made worse by the fact that they never apologized or expressed remorse in any way. Emotionally, I felt like I was getting beat down over and over again, but this time I was doing the kicking by running the non-stop movie in my head.

The struggle was real. I was stuck. I was still angry and hurt. I was not moving forward.

I could hear my mother's voice, "Forgiveness will help you stop being angry."

But, how do you forgive someone if they don't even ask to be forgiven? Yes, I realized there was part of me that believed it was easier to forgive if someone showed remorse for their actions and asked to be forgiven. But that means they are still in control and have power over you. I finally got sick and tired of feeling powerless and angry all the time. I desperately needed to be released from the self-imposed prison.

My next epiphany (although deep down, I always knew) was realizing that I could give myself the gift of forgiveness any time I chose to. How the people connected to the school assault hurt me had no real bearing on whether I was going to release myself from that emotional hell and move forward. Forgiving them was going to set me free. Forgiving them allowed me to regain my power. And I believe, without question, that you should always be the most powerful person in your own life.

Over the years, I have learned to forgive many individuals. But, there was one person I really struggled with forgiving, more than anyone else. I really questioned whether they even deserved to be forgiven.

That person was me.

I would sometimes beat myself up for making a mistake and then continue to "should on myself" after the fact. I should have known better. I should have turned right instead of left. I should have made a different choice. And the list goes on. The constant "shoulding" can cause tremendous judgement leading to guilt and shame and erosion of our self-worth.

I recall a time when I went down that slippery slope of self-judgment. A few years ago, I had a very negative renovation experience. The contractors I hired caused a lot of damage and did not honor their word, costing me thousands of dollars in repairs. I really beat myself up for hiring them. I was actually punishing myself, over and over again. *Shame on me. I should have known better. Why did I hire them?*

Now, did I intentionally set out to hurt myself or cause damage to my home? Absolutely not. But, I acted like I did. I would never let a friend treat themselves that way. I would encourage them to have grace and forgive themselves. So, why didn't I extend the same grace to myself?

I was sharing the renovation adventure with a friend, and she asked, "Why did you hire those guys?" (as if I knew how it would turn out). I looked at her and said, "I woke up that day and asked, 'How could I royally screw myself over,' made a list, and hiring those contractors was at the top of the list." Of course, that wasn't true, even though I was behaving like it was.

Yes, forgiveness is a tool for freedom! It is a gift you give yourself.

It has always been easier to forgive others before myself. However, when I thought about the intention behind the action, the tide started to shift. Realizing I never intended to cause harm to myself or my home allowed me to have more grace with myself.

We all make mistakes. We are human.

What do you
need to forgive
yourself for?

Chapter 10
CREATION

> *"The best way to predict the future is to create it."*
> – Bryant H. McGill

> *"Don't wait for it to get better. Get better at it."*
> – Eleni Anastos

CREATION

It is very clear to me how actively I have been creating my life, post-school assault. However, now knowing what I know from lessons learned, I realize creation has been an active ingredient in my life from day one and in yours' as well.

I was very blessed to be raised in my maternal grandparents' home, along with my loving mother. They created an environment of love and acceptance, and they encouraged individuality. I recall my YiaYia, Papou and Mom often saying, "You can be or do anything you want, just set your mind to it and be willing to do the work." They reinforced that working towards my dreams may not be easy, but would definitely be worth it. And, I was always encouraged to learn and grow.

Often after school, I would sit at the kitchen table and listen to my grandfather sharing his pearls of wisdom. One afternoon, when talking about growing up and moving through life, he said, "You may lose things as you get older … a job, car, money, etc. But, no one can ever take away your education or experience. You can always begin again."

Yes, they taught me that you are the creator of your own life, and I am forever grateful for that foundation.

I must admit, however, that there were periods of time when I strayed from that foundation and found a home in the illusion of safety and security. It became quite acceptable to not always go after dreams. I had a good life and was content, but deep down, I wanted more. So, why didn't I aggressively pursue my dreams? I went down a rabbit hole and convinced myself that I was OK with being OK. Sadly, there was a lot of company in that space. Instead of lifting each other up, we made a silent pact to acknowledge each other for "not going for it." There was a definite camaraderie and sharing of why things wouldn't work.

It's too hard.

It's too late to start something new.

Things are fine just the way they are.

What if you make a mistake?

Yes, I had real dreams inside of me, but wasn't taking action.

Maybe I thought it would be too hard. Maybe I feared looking foolish and making mistakes. Maybe I thought it was too late. Maybe I was letting too many other voices rent space in my head.

Did I stop creating?

Of course, I realize now I was ALWAYS creating, just not always in the direction of my heart's desire.

Life is always about growth and expansion.

In *The Science of Getting Rich*, Wallace Wattles discusses "The Impression of Increase:"

"Increase is what all men and all women are seeking; it is the urge of the Formless Intelligence within them, seeking fuller expression."

Wanting more is fundamental in all of us (more money, more friendship, more food, more travel, more knowledge, etc.), so what stops us from seeking that which we desire?

The answer is always within.

I had to admit that I allowed fear and doubt to have more power than my heart's desire. I was not purposefully using creation to expand my life in a positive direction.

In which direction do you want to see growth and expansion?

Settling serves no one.

Don't allow the fear of making mistakes stop you from stepping up to the plate.

Get in the game. We all know you miss 100% of the shots you don't take. Be grateful for your mistakes. They can be valuable sources of insight, telling you where you need to grow. Analyze the situation and gather the necessary feedback to correct your course. You will learn what to do differently the next time. A mistake does not have to stop you! Keep moving forward and keep taking action while staying focused on your desired outcome.

We've all used some type of navigating system (GPS) when traveling. You get in the car and enter your final destination. With modern technology, you are able to view the entire route, step by step. However, this is rarely true in matters of life. Many are held back by fear of the unknown and refuse to get out of the starting gate without knowing every step on the path. Learn to embrace that the way will be shown to you, when you begin taking action. Once you are on the path, you may make a wrong turn or come across an unexpected obstacle that takes you off the designated route. Does the GPS system say, "You're screwed. You're stuck. You have to stay in this spot forever"?

NO ... it says "recalculating" or "rerouting."

Allow those mistakes or obstacles to guide you to an even better route. The fear of making a mistake will only serve to keep you stuck if you allow it. Let the mistake be a lesson, not a life sentence.

Let's be honest, problems and obstacles are a normal part of life. We all face them. Shit happens!

Are you expanding the problem by focusing on it more? Where do you want your creative energy to be focused?

Yes, you are a creator.

A strong desire to get to your destination (achieving that goal) can help you to push through any problem or obstacle, so focus your creative energy on your desired outcome. The choice is yours.

I am back to being a conscious creator and owning 100% responsibility for my life! And, if things don't initially work out as desired, I will recalculate and continue to create!

And, I will continue to learn and grow and trust in my ability to move forward. If you have faith in yourself, you will be unstoppable because the real power is always within. Creation IS your power source.

In the Wizard of Oz, Dorothy was so concerned and worried when the wizard left, believing she did not have the power or ability to get back to Kansas without him. Glinda, the Good Witch, explained to Dorothy what many of us fail to realize: "You've always had the power."

So, I ask again, what do you really desire to have in your life?

Protect Your Dreams

I am so grateful to now have realized just how much of a role creation has played in my life and everyone else's.

I recall a conversation with a young soul (late twenties) who was very excited about launching her new business. She was thrilled when thinking about the people she was going to serve. You could feel Lisa's energy when she spoke about putting herself out there and making money.

She shared her business dream with some friends and relatives, many of whom immediately shot her down. *It's not viable. You're not going to make any money. Where will you find clients?*

You could see her physically shrink down. Lisa began to question herself. *Can I really do this? Is it viable? Am I making a mistake?*

It is perfectly OK if others do not believe in your dreams. Most likely, they are projecting their own limiting beliefs. You don't have to let them rent space in your head!

Your YES has to be bigger than their NO.

If you have a strong desire to create something in your life, to be, do or have more, tap into that and push through. Desire always finds a way. Connect to it on an emotional level. Why is it important to you? Fuel the desire. Focus on the feeling of having accomplished it already! Become crystal clear with what you want and let that image be your resource for energy and motivation to keep moving forward. Picture a dog on the wrong side of the fence from his treat or when a child is relentless in their pursuit of a present or toy.

Be protective of your dreams/goals/desires like you would of anything that has tremendous value for you. And, be very mindful of who you share them with. Not everyone will have the ability to accept and support your vision. I know this can be challenging, especially with those who are closest to us.

You are gambling with your own success when you allow a challenge or fear of rejection to stop you.

Success requires that we do our best repeatedly, day after day. We must cultivate positive habits that will keep us moving forward.

Make the decision that you are no longer willing to settle for less than you desire, regardless of what others may think.

Will it take hard work? Yes! Will it be worth it? Yes!

Other people will always project their shit onto you. If you allow doubt from an outside source into your head, it will steal your dreams.

Yes, you should always own your own shit, but never own anyone else's.

It's your life!

Keep CREATING what you desire!

Passion Takes Form

I have learned that one of the many gifts of creation is giving form to your passion and enthusiasm. It is true spirit flowing to you and through you.

Suzanne was an incredibly enthusiastic student teacher and very passionate about making a difference. The adolescents I had worked with earlier in my teaching career were identified as emotionally impaired, and many of the issues they faced could be overwhelming. Maintaining a degree of structure was necessary to keep students focused on learning. However, this was far from an easy task, especially for a student teacher with no prior experience.

Suzanne had the best of intentions but was having an especially difficult time one afternoon. She kept trying to focus two students on their assignments, and they wanted nothing to do with it. It did not matter what Suzanne said or did. It did not matter that she had the best of intentions. The students would not comply. They also became quite verbally disrespectful – chewing her up and spitting her out. She was overwhelmed.

Suzanne came to me after school that day, with tears in her eyes and begged, "Please tell me it gets easier." I sat next to her, held her hands, looked into her eyes and said, "Suzanne, the shit gets worse!" She began sobbing uncontrollably. I continued, "Don't wait for it to get better. You get better at it. That is what will make the difference."

Can you control everything that happens around you? Absolutely not. Can you control how you respond and move through the situation? Yes. You have a choice. You are a creator.

Focused Creative Energy

A neighbor once commented, "You are so lucky you work from home and can make your own schedule." I responded, "Luck had nothing to do with it." I created and continue to create the life I desire.

When is the last time you thought about what you really desire in life?

Do you allow external factors to control your vision and dreams? Are you lowering your standards to meet circumstances?

My mother passed away at age eighty-four. For several years prior to her death, she was more than legally blind, on oxygen 24/7, wheelchair-bound and in constant pain. BUT, I fondly recall her saying, "Every day you wake up is a chance for a dream to come true." My mother didn't use her creative energy to focus on problems. Lula knew that if she could imagine it in her mind, it was still possible for it to materialize in her life. My mom never let age or circumstance stop her from believing and dreaming. Thank you for that beautiful gift, Mom. That spirit has helped me through many difficult times and helped me realize, we are still creators, even when in pain.

Yes, embracing your ability to create has tremendous power. When the energy flows into our minds, it will take the shape of what we are thinking about. The image in our minds then moves into form, and our external world becomes a reflection of our internal thoughts.

It is the creative process. Energy must take the shape of what it flows through. Energy constantly moves to us and through us and contains the knowledge of the Universe. You cannot create something that hasn't been seen.

The reality is we are in a constant state of creation, whether you choose to work with it or not. But, you do need to ask yourself important questions. *Am I creating the life I want*, or am I creating the life I don't want?

Confusion only arises when your desire isn't clear. This opens the door for doubt to creep into your mind. We all know that doubt is a dream killer.

So, if you find yourself saying "I don't have..." "I don't know...," be aware that doubt has entered your mind, and refocus on your vision. Keep that internal image clear to help drive you forward.

Focus. Attach emotion. Put energy into it. Write out your goals and read them out loud several times a day. Spend time visualizing yourself already possessing what you desire.

We must exercise our bodies to keep them strong. The same principle applies to our desires.

Focusing your energy on what you want will also help you reject negative thoughts or images and keep your motivation on track. We already know that what we focus on expands and our external world always represents what is happening internally. The choice is yours'. You are a creator!

The Universe will hold nothing back from you. Everything you need is already here. Remember what Glinda the Good Witch told Dorothy?

Focus on what IS possible while developing the habits and skills necessary to bring you what you desire. You will be open and ready for the right opportunities.

So, what do you really want and why do you want it?

Honestly, you would not have a true desire for something if the possibility for it coming into your life didn't exist. Spirit will always guide you to move in a positive direction for growth, while fear can keep you paralyzed. This opens the door for doubt and confusion to creep in, which only serves to keep you stuck. You need clarity and focus.

I was speaking with an entrepreneur who kept hesitating to officially launch her business. She was questioning herself.

Can I start connecting with potential clients about my business before I have a website? Before I have a perfect logo design and business cards? Before I have every single marketing tool in place?

YES! The answer is yes to all the above. My first coaching client was very successful in business but did not apply the same principles to himself on a personal level. He was looking for guidance and support to achieve all of his life goals. We were discussing what it would look like to work together when Bill asked if I had a website or at least a brochure he could review. I had neither and responded, "No, I do not yet, but I'm right here, Bill. What do you need to know?"

He hired me on the spot.

Had I believed I needed everything in place before I could be of service, I would have missed a wonderful opportunity. I was already a coach, and I decided to move forward (even without all of the bells and whistles).

Are you stuck in your "before"?

Before I move forward, I need _____.
Before I make a change, I have to _____.
Before I can be happy, I need to _____.

Decide you are going to move forward. Decide you are going to change. Decide you are going to be happy.

The decision always comes first. Nothing will happen unless you commit and take action.

Actively Creating

We are always in a constant state of creation. Are you purposefully using that energy?

Are you creating a life you want or don't want?

Haven't we all said at one time or another, "I wish things were different" regarding some area of life, yet continued to make the same choices?

Perhaps you have fallen into a coma of complacency. We know real growth only happens outside of your comfort zone. Perhaps you have lost sight of your ability to create.

Or, have you been lowering your standards to meet circumstances? You can rise above the conditions of your environment.

The hardest part of change is not making the same choices over and over again.

Einstein clearly defined insanity: *Doing the same thing over and over again and expecting different results.*

Be willing to change. Know that you are a creator. Become a conscious creator.

And you don't have to be broken to want to be better.

Technology constantly sends updates with software upgrades. This doesn't mean your phone or laptop isn't working, but it does mean there is room for improvement. It's up to you to download the new software. When you embrace being a conscious creator, you become the programmer for your own internal operating system. Sometimes a strong reboot is necessary to keep moving forward. It helps to clear out what is keeping you from operating at an optimal level.

Reboot – Realign – Refocus

There are times in life where we must release things (people, parts of your environment, bad attitude, etc.) of a lower nature to make room for things of a higher nature.

Life is always about growth and expansion.

Settling serves no one.

You are the creator of your life.

Create Opportunities

Dave Bing represents an excellent example of purposefully creating in life, and I am forever grateful that I "created" an opportunity to meet him.

He was a successful NBA athlete who played for the Detroit Pistons and later became even more successful as an entrepreneur. He built a business that employed countless people in the city of Detroit and was earning over 600 Million dollars the year we met.

Dave Bing was active in business groups and would often speak at live events, sharing his story and definition of success.

My oldest brother Peter was a BIG fan (and so was I).

I came across an opportunity to hear Dave speak in person. The event was held in an auditorium at a local college. There were at least 500 people in attendance (a mix of entrepreneurs, business executives and long-time basketball fans). Dave recalled a story from his college days. It was the first day of training for the new season. The team had won a national championship the previous year and reported to practice still feeling "quite proud of themselves." The coach quickly chimed in, "That was last year. What are you going to do now?"

It reminded me of my grandfather (the successful restauranteur) saying, "We are only as good as our last meal."

As I listened to Dave talk, I kept wishing my brother Peter could have been there with me. He died only a few months prior.

After the speech, everyone filed out of the

auditorium to the parking lot. As I was walking back to my car, I kept thinking, "Peter would have loved to meet him." So, I turned right around and went back into the auditorium. Dave was still on stage with his entourage (bodyguards included) all around. It was clearly stated at the end of his speech that he would not be able to meet with anyone individually.

I hesitated for a moment and then said to myself, "What's the worst thing that could happen? They could say, "Get that crazy bitch out of here," and I was OK with that.

So, I marched down to the stage and walked quickly in between two of his guards. I went directly to Dave and told him how much his talk resonated with me and shared the story of my grandfather.

Mr. Bing thanked me and asked, "What do you do (professionally)?" I said I helped businesses get money when the banks said no (accounts receivable financing, equipment leasing, etc.). He asked if I had a card. With a slightly shaky voice (I couldn't believe this was really happening), I responded, "Yes sir," and handed him my business card. Dave said he wanted to have me come into his company to discuss the funding work I did.

Sure, the CEO of a 600-million-dollar company was going to invite little ole me, a small independent consultant in for a conversation.

It didn't matter. I was thrilled that I got to meet him. I drove home, feeling my brother Peter's energy and spirit. We met Dave Bing together! But that wasn't the ending!

The next day I received a phone call: "Hi Eleni, this is Sally, Dave Bing's secretary, and he would like you to come in for a meeting with one of our executive Vice Presidents." What? Was I dreaming? I started jumping up and down like I had scored the winning basket in a championship game!

I went to The Bing Group a few days later. It was all very real, and Dave Bing was a man of his word.

Fast forward a few years and Dave Bing was now mayor of Detroit. He was speaking at a Chamber of Commerce event, with hundreds of people in attendance. When it was time for Q&A, a gentleman stood up and asked about a particular city service that was not being delivered in a timely fashion in his neighborhood. Dave asked for the gentleman's phone number because he wanted to investigate and follow up directly with him when he had the answer. The man in the audience said "Sure, but why bother, it's not like the mayor is actually going to follow up." I jumped to my feet and shouted, "Yes, he will. Dave Bing is a man of his word." Dave looked over at me with familiar eyes and thanked me for standing up for him. We had the chance to speak during the next break.

Meeting Dave Bing remains a favorite memory, and I am grateful that I allowed myself to "create" that experience.

Being purposefully focused on creation has given me many good memories, and I look forward to many more.

Do you believe that you can be a powerful creator in your own life?

Or, are you waiting for life to happen to you? Of course, there will be circumstances/situations/obstacles (some quite painful) beyond our control. But, how we choose to respond IS and always will be within our control.

The school assault (and subsequent aftermath) was beyond my control, and it was an incredibly painful and difficult time for me. I felt completely lost. I remember desperately wanting to feel better and to just move through it.

What I didn't initially realize was that I needed to "grow through it."

I have heard countless times, "I'm sure you wish that never happened," and I admit, there were times I allowed my mind to dwell there, serving no useful purpose. If I continued to focus my energy in that direction, I would not be able to grow through it.

Life is about expansion and growth. The direction of that expansion and growth is within your power as a creator.

Yes, the school assault happened and was extremely painful – physically, mentally and emotionally.

When I got to the point of not being able to even imagine a brighter future, I had to change. I decided to change. I needed to create something different.

The assault showed me that I had not always been purposefully creating my best life.

There really was a purpose for the pain.

And now, I do not fear pain; instead, I allow it to catalyze my growth.

I am back to knowing and believing that I can

and will CREATE the life I desire and deserve. I am living with even greater purpose.

I own my life and am 100% responsible because I took my power back.

Are you listening?

You can control your life.

You are a creator.

What could you create
if you believed you had
the ability to do so?

REINVENTION
MOVING FORWARD

It is time to paint your own picture.

Even prior to the Pandemic, countless individuals have dealt with major challenges and obstacles that have required a shift in perspective, a need for reinvention to get their lives back on track.

Yes, redefining who you are and your purpose in life can be daunting, especially if you try to do it all alone.

I'm here to help you with that process.

So, let's connect the dots between all that you have experienced and how that has prepared you to create an amazing new chapter. (Because the shit you have gone through and survived can be a roadmap for others – their survival guide.)

It's time to thrive again and get fired up about your future!

And remember, you are not starting over from scratch. You are starting over from experience.

What do you really want? Really?

Self-imposed parameters need not apply. Kick those limiting beliefs to the curb! You have found purpose in your pain, lessons that have allowed you to grow. So, let's get real!

What do you think about in your secret thoughts? Is there something more that you want to be, do or have?

It's your time!

Here is the *3-Step Formula* I created and used to reinvent my life and have used to help countless clients to do the same.

1. Take a "Circle of Life" Inventory

Before you plan your future, it is important to know exactly where you're starting. Much like the GPS system we use in our cars, you cannot be given the right guidance and directions if you don't know exactly where you are starting from.

Rate your level of satisfaction in each of the following major life areas (scale of 1-10):

Family/friends; money; physical health, mental health, physical environment, fun/recreation, career/life purpose, spiritual alignment.

REINVENTION: MOVING FORWARD

Be honest about how you currently feel, while reflecting on what you would like to see going forward.

2. Make a Personal Venn Diagram (3 lists)

Most people probably first learned of a traditional Venn diagram in school, perhaps in a math class. You see circles with different categories, overlapping to compare similarities and differences between the categories.

A personal Venn diagram is used to help individuals focus in on their own strengths, abilities, and experiences while seeing similarities and differences in those areas.

a) List everything you truly enjoy doing regardless of circumstance (working out, cooking, writing, playing an instrument, etc.).

b) List all of the things you are a rock star at (time to give yourself credit for your talents, skillsets and experiences).

c) List all of the things that people instinctively come to you for (family, friends or colleagues know you are the person who can help them with x,y,z).

As you review and compare the three circles, highlight the commonalities in the middle. What you see in the center can be used as the catalyst to your new beginning.

Example: I worked with a talented individual, who was very successful in sales, but not truly happy and wanted to reinvent his life going forward. I had him do the personal Venn diagram with the circles listing what he really enjoyed doing, things he was great at, and the things people always came to him for. We instantly saw that writing, communication and connecting with people was the common ground in all three areas. Now he is focusing his energy on writing. We all know that everyone has a story, and he is magical at helping people share their journey in writing. But, it really didn't dawn on him until we did the Venn diagram.

I had a lengthy career in education, and my own personal Venn Diagram clearly showed communication, problem-solving, strategy and public speaking as the common ground in the center, which all lent themselves perfectly to becoming a professional coach.

3. Reverse Engineer to Create Your Roadmap

First, project out one year, five years, ten years, etc. and imagine living your happy and prosperous reinvented life. Build that vision out! What does your day-to-day life include? Add specific, quantifiable details to make the vision tangible.

Since you have already begun with the end in mind, reverse engineer to create the roadmap that will take you there.

Did you move? If you see yourself living somewhere different, what did it take to relocate? Did you have to buy or sell property? Are you renting?

Did you release people or things from your life? Remember, sometimes it is necessary to release things of a lower nature to make room for things of a higher nature.

Did you start a new career or business? Did it take any additional education/training/certifications?

It's great to have that image of what you

want your life to be like, but you still have to do the work to get there! People talk a lot about visualization and making vision boards, which are great, but not successful without ACTION. You still have to be ready and willing to do the work and capitalize on opportunities to get there!

Imagine sitting across the street from your dream home. You can really visualize yourself in there, see family, even see yourself hosting a barbecue in the backyard, BUT you don't take it any further! How tasty is that barbecue when it's only in your head? Get off your ass and move!

You have to reverse engineer to come up with the action steps that will put you in that house!

I began this book with one of my favorite phrases, and I'm called to share it again.

I didn't come this far, to only come this far!

Regardless of age, ask yourself: is there something else you want to be, do or have?

Skillsets and experience can be applied in multiple arenas. Again, you are not starting from scratch, you are starting from experience.

Many people align themselves solely with what they have always done, But I'm here to tell you ...

It may be all that you've ever done, but it is not all that you are!

Purposeful reinvention is the foundation for living your best life.

And please reach out for support. None of us is meant to do this alone.

Your next chapter can be one of your best! Here's to your fired-up future!!!

I'm cheering you on!

Dear Reader,

It is hard to believe that I've come to the end of the book. But, in many beautiful ways, I am just beginning. And that is my wish for you too.

So, thank you for joining me on this journey. I am grateful that you chose to spend time with me.

I wrote this book during the adventure known as 2020, and it has definitely been my year of purposeful reinvention. A big part of that was rebranding my business under my own name, Eleni Anastos.

However, there is a little more to the backstory that I want to share with you. Branding a business under your own name sounds simple enough (countless people do it), but for me, it was anything but simple.

For several years I couldn't even Google my own name. I physically and emotionally could not bring myself to do it. I clearly recall the last time I did type my name into the search bar, prior to 2020. At the top of page one appeared, "Teacher sues district over alleged assault."

Reading those words caused every painful emotion connected to that experience to come flooding back. I cried. I hid under the covers. I just couldn't bear to see my name in print, let alone really put myself out there.

But, fortunately, I did not quit on myself. I kept moving forward with my life and coaching business. A dear friend recently asked why I didn't quit on myself. I said, "I know, with every fiber of my being, that I am meant to help people live their best lives. If I quit, I won't be able to reach the people I am meant to serve."

I forged on, grew my business and really began putting myself out there. Over the last couple of years, I have appeared on numerous podcasts, radio shows and streaming networks, and this year (2020) on national television. When my dear friend Kimberly suggested I brand under my own name, I hesitated, but not for long. I knew it was the right thing to do. It was my time. So, I Googled my name, and the first couple of pages were filled with media guest appearances and other activities related to my business.

The school assault article was in the middle of page three. A few years ago, that would have taken me out, crying and hiding under the covers. But this time my response was quite different. It didn't take me out, but served as fuel to propel me even farther forward. That article will always be out there. It's a part of my journey, but it no longer controls me!

The process of finding purpose in the pain sure wasn't easy, but damn, it was worth it. Even as I write this, I am feeling more empowered.

It is my sincere hope that you don't quit on yourself! You deserve to live your best life!

Purposeful reinvention is the foundation that can make your next chapter one of your best.

With Love and Gratitude,

Eleni

P.S. Please remember, you don't have to go through this journey alone. Reach out for support! I'm still cheering you on!

Please enjoy this audio series:

www.myreinventedlifereaderbonus.com

www.elenianastos.com

Insider Access

SCAN ME

BOOK CLUB DISCUSSION QUESTIONS

1. What did you like best about this book?

2. Share a favorite quote from the book. Why did this quote stand out?

3. What feelings did this book evoke for you?

4. What did you learn from reading this book?

5. If you got the chance to ask the author one question, what would it be?

6. What do you feel was the author's purpose in writing this book?

7. What new questions do you now have about this subject after reading this book?

8. What aspect of the story did you most relate to?

9. What surprised you about this book or the subject?

10. What was your one take-away from the book that you will use in your life moving forward?